DIEGO COSTA
THE ART OF WAR

DIEGO COSTA
THE ART OF WAR

FRAN GUILLÉN

First published in Great Britain in 2015 by
ARENA SPORT
An imprint of Birlinn Limited
West Newington House
10 Newington Road
Edinburgh
EH9 1QS

www.arenasportbooks.co.uk

Published in association with
BACKPAGE PRESS
www.backpagepress.co.uk

ISBN: 978-1-909715-29-5
eBook ISBN: 978-0-85790-857-5

First published in Spain in 2014 by Al Poste Ediciones as
Diego Costa : El Arte de la Guerra

British Library Cataloguing-in-Publication Data
A catalogue record for this book is available on request from the
British Library.

Designed and typeset by Polaris Publishing, Edinburgh

Printed and bound by Clays St Ives

For my parents, without whom nothing would be possible

For all those who, like Diego, will not rest until they make their dreams come true

CONTENTS

PROLOGUE

SUMMER 2014. Cobham, 15 miles south-west of London. Chelsea's training ground.

Oscar is looking for three of his team-mates. He wants to introduce them to someone. Diego Costa has arrived for his first day as a Chelsea player and he has something he wants to say. He doesn't have much English yet, but Oscar, a fellow Brazilian, has helped him with the words. He's been practicing a single, short sentence. Actually, a mission statement.

The last time John Terry, Gary Cahill, Branislav Ivanović and Nemanja Matić had seen Costa was at Stamford Bridge, as he shook their hands and left the pitch, on his way to the Champions League final after Atlético Madrid's 3-1 victory over Chelsea.

Costa had won and scored the penalty that put his team 2-1 ahead, but in neither that match, nor the first leg of the semi-final, a 0-0 draw in the Spanish capital, had he been at his fearsome best. Chelsea's muscular defence had certainly not been devastated by Costa. The trail of destruction he had cast across Spain in season 2013-14 had not stretched to England.

As Costa was substituted late on in London, the Chelsea fans sang: 'Diego Costa, we'll see you next year.' The striker's next destination was no big secret.

But since then Costa's stock had plummeted. A hamstring injury all but ended his participation in both the successful title run-in and the last-gasp defeat in the Champions League final. Then, at the World Cup, his sterile performances as Brazil jeered his every touch became one of the motifs of Spain's abdication as world champions. Was this really the new Didier Drogba? Or just another in the long line of strikers who had failed to fill Drogba's boots at Chelsea?

Oscar introduces Terry, Cahill, Ivanović and Matić to Diego Costa. They shake hands, then Costa straightens up and delivers his pitch in heavily-accented, halting English.

"I go to war. You come with me."

It's funny, and they all laugh a little. But as the defenders head off to begin training, they share a look. They have found their man. Their warrior centre-forward.

It. Is. On.

1

THE STREET FOOTBALLER

*'Only one who is thoroughly acquainted with the evils
of war is able to thoroughly understand the profitable
way of carrying it out'*

Sun Tzu, *The Art of War*

DIEGO DA SILVA COSTA arrived in the world on
October 7, 1988, in Lagarto, the third-largest city
(with just over 100,000 inhabitants) in the state of
Sergipe, north-east Brazil. His mother, Josileide Costa,
was a nursery nurse, and his father, José de Jesús Silva
(aka Zeinha), was a farm worker and casual Sunday
footballer who had always dreamed of having a player
in the family. He also had two siblings: brother Jair
(named after the Brazilian legend Jairzinho; Costa
himself was named after Diego Maradona), and a
sister, Talita.

Costa's birthplace is known for cattle farming, some
industry and agricultural production – mainly oranges,
tobacco and passion fruit. "Nowadays you could almost
call it a bustling metropolis. They built a university
campus here and the city expanded as a result," explains
Prefeitinho, Costa's childhood friend. "But back then it
was much more rural."

The young Costa was a football obsessive from the
very first, inspired by his father and uncles who refused

to accept that dreams could not become reality, even in a place like Lagarto.

"It was a poor city and it would have been easy to moan about our lack of opportunities," says Prefeitinho. "But Diego didn't think like that. He could easily have gone down the wrong track or at the very least given up on his early dreams. But he believed in his own potential. He knew what he wanted and he worked himself into the ground to get to where he wanted to go. He knew he was talented and he set out to prove it."

Costa's first experience of football away from the street or the piece of land he played on at his grandparents' house was the Boula de Ouro school, a social project which he now helps fund and which provides underprivileged kids with free training. Aged nine, he would set out on the 40-minute walk to the vacant wasteground where the rather chaotic sessions took place. Nowadays things are better organised and the school provides football training to 200 kids aged between eight and 17 who play on proper pitches provided by the local council.

Sometimes Costa cycled to football and on those occasions he would take along his equally football-mad neighbour Mário César, who was speech-and-hearing impaired.

"Diego insisted on bringing along this deaf and dumb kid," smiles Flávio Augusto Machado, 'Flavinho', his first coach who is still coaching today, with his whistle in his hand and an Atlético Madrid cap on his head. "I wasn't happy and I said so. Mário just couldn't understand what I said, but Diego was always there to translate for him."

In 2013, in a fitting tribute to their shared childhood experiences, Costa presented Mário César with a motorbike.

The player's warrior-like approach to football was evident from the first.

"I have never coached anyone who fought so hard on the football pitch," Flavinho recalls. "He was a great kid but he was determined to win. He would settle for nothing less."

"As a boy he was no different from the player you see today," adds Prefeitinho. "For him there was no such thing as a lost ball. Other players see a ball that looks out of reach and they let it go. Not this guy. He has no fear, he wants that ball, he wants to score and he'll fight tooth and nail to do so."

Costa's father agrees. "He never liked losing and whenever he did, he'd come off in a foul mood. He'd pull at his jersey and stare at the ground in silence all the way home."

It was Papa Costa who was the first to spot how special his son was. "I just knew I'd be watching him on television one day," Zeinha recalls.

Flavinho was also alert to his potential. "He was

3

much taller than the other kids and you could see that he had something extra."

"By the time he was nine he was playing with the 11-year-olds," his mother explains, "and by 16 he was very mature, already an adult mentally. He always excelled. If he was playing in the school team in a competition, they always won."

"I remember they told us to run round this plantation," explains Junior Menezes, another close friend. "Whenever the coach wasn't looking, Diego and I would always take the short cuts so that we didn't get too tired. We were just kids and always wanted to get back to playing as quickly as possible. He was completely obsessed about football." As well as remaining good friends, Costa and Junior are today partners in the football school they fund.

Economic imperatives dictated that Costa was relatively old before he began to play organised football with a local club, Fluminense da Horta. "He captained the only city club to become junior champions [in 1998]," recalls Prefeitinho. "Diego attended the 15th anniversary celebrations of that win, although he couldn't play in the game. He was the best player from that era and the one who ended up as a professional."

Costa also had an unsuccessful trial for Atlético Clube Lagartense, in his home city, but it was in São Paulo that he would eventually get his first break and embark on a long and twisting path to the top of world football.

"The family moved to São Paulo when I was 14 and my brother started to go out partying at night," recounts Costa. "I wanted to give up football so that I could earn some money. My dad would give me a couple of notes here and there, but it wasn't really enough and sometimes I had to stay in because I couldn't face going out on a date and letting the girl pay."

Costa took a job with his uncle and the pair of them would drive a truck to the Paraguay border, where they would stock up on goods to sell in the Galería Pagé shopping centre.

Costa explains: "Whenever my uncle met anyone from football, he would mention my name. He'd say, 'I've got this nephew who's super-talented...' But I didn't want to play football if it stopped me earning money, especially since my uncle tended to pay me more than I'd actually earned, and I had no living costs because I stayed with him at the time. I saved up and bought myself a motorbike so that I could visit Lagarto, although my mother did everything she could to get me to sell it."

Uncle Edson, however, had a stubborn streak and was to play a key role at this stage in Costa's career. He insisted on taking his nephew for trials and eventually one club expressed an interest. Barcelona Esportivo Capela de Ibiúna was owned by a local businessman whose policy was to invest in young players. The team's matches were therefore well attended by scouts.

"We had to play in a competition in Minas Gerais. I wasn't keen because I wanted to work but my uncle insisted that I go and told me that he'd pay me anyway. So I went. Although in the end he didn't pay me after all!"

He performed well in the *azulgrana* strip (in fact, the club's name was not inspired by FC Barcelona, but by another local team, Sociedade Esportiva Barcelona) particularly considering that despite being 16 this was his first experience of playing with a professionally organised club. The player is clear about the reasons for his late arrival into professional football: "There was no infrastructure, no resources in the town where I grew up."

The club's directors selected a few players to train with the well-established Yuracan de Itajubá, famous in Brazil as the club of Pelé's father, Dondinho, who scored five headers in an historic 6-2 win over the team's big rivals, Smart Futebol Clube, in 1938. Pelé's old man always claimed that this was the only record of his that his son had never managed to beat.

Costa spent eight months playing friendlies and one under-17 tournament for Itajubá. According to the Yuracan president, Amauri Graciani, Costa "was already emerging as a special player. We used him in the box as a centre-forward although he instinctively preferred to move about more and go down the pitch to get the ball. He was always looking for a goal, but he also caused a lot of trouble."

Having returned to Ibiúna, the youngster was about to play the game that would change the course of his life.

"[Costa's agent] Jorge Mendes tells me that he spotted him in the Taça de São Paulo, a tournament they play in January down there," says Jesús García Pitarch, the man responsible for later bringing Costa to Atlético in his role as the Madrid club's director of football. "It is an under-18 tournament and the final is always played in the Pacaembú [Corinthians' stadium]. It's a huge event and a big party for the whole city. Scouts and coaches from the big clubs always come to the final, but even in the early stages you see unbelievable players and there are a lot of clubs who do very well out of it. Even though Diego managed to get himself sent off in the first match – remarkable! – he had already caught someone's eye."

"I remember that I shouldn't even have been playing that match because I had already been suspended for four months for slapping an opponent and then giving the referee a bit of lip when he showed me the red card," recalls Costa. "I've no idea if someone had been pulling strings behind the scenes, but I ended up playing anyway."

After the final whistle, a representative of Mendes

approached Costa and talked about the possibility of playing in Europe.

"The minute I came off I talked to Mendes' representative and they signed me up to go to Sporting de Braga. I didn't hesitate for a moment because I knew that Jorge was behind the offer and that he was pretty much the best in the world."

The idea was less well received at home. "When I signed for Braga, my dad and uncle took the contract to São Caetano, who offered the same deal for me to stay. My dad was worried that I would end up like the boys who are offered the chance to play in Europe only to be let down at the last minute. But I had given my word and in the end he started to believe that the Braga offer was genuine."

It was a bittersweet prospect for the family, but Costa was firm. "If you don't let me go, I'll run away anyway," he told his mother, who understood that her youngest son was realising a dream long cherished by the whole family. "My mum cried a lot when I left," recalls Costa.

His brother Jair also had hopes of turning professional. He had trained with Diego and had had a three-month trial with Sociedad Deportiva Salvatierra, a small club based in Álava, without success. Today he recognises that "I just wasn't as committed as my brother". Prefeitinho goes further. "Jair was probably better than Diego, but he was more relaxed about things. He didn't have the same level of focus. He still plays, but he's always lacked the persistence you need. They played in the same team and were always rowing. One of them would have to be taken off so that things didn't get out of hand. Jair was a better player, he was slender and fast on his feet. Diego was a powerhouse though."

The same indomitable Costa set out from Lagarto. "When you play street football you learn to be smarter than the rest," he explained. "I made no attempt to control myself and was always ready for a bit of aggro. My mates and I would often end the game in tears."

Looking back, he remembers street games in which he would often be up against boys who were "at least as good or even better" than him.

Those who knew him at the time remember him fondly. Prefeitinho says: "He's a brilliant guy and he hasn't changed a bit since those days. He's always been shy and likes to be on good terms with everyone. He was never the kind of kid to hang about on the streets causing trouble. Not because he was deliberately keeping his head down, it's just the way he is naturally. He's a down-to-earth kind of person who is reserved and a bit shy. Even when he was a little kid he always picked the right kind of mates and made good choices. And he has never forgotten where he's come from. Nunes, who was also from Sergipe and who played for Brazil in the 80s, used to say he was from Bahia [a neighbouring state]. Not Diego. He always says that he's from Lagarto and tries to visit his soccer school whenever they invite him. He's very sociable whenever he's home and makes a point of visiting people who are sick."

Costa has said he will retire to Lagarto, and would like to end his career playing in Brazil, probably at Palmeiras, the club he supports. Whether or not that is how it plays out, and despite the many stops on his road to greatness, this is a footballer who is unlikely to forget his roots. When he returns, to his family or the school he funds, and sees the statue of the giant stone lizard that greets visitors to the city, he is reminded of where his extraordinary journey began.

2
THE LEAGUE OF HONOUR

*'If we wish to fight, we can force the enemy to fight
even if he is protected by a high wall and a deep moat'*

Sun Tzu, *The Art of War*

A NEW CONTINENT, a new style of football, a new life.

"Sure, I cried a bit but I always told my mum, who can be a bit emotional, that everything was great. I was very young and because all the documentation took a while to sort out, I was only training for the first six months. After that I got to play matches."

Although he had family members with him for the first eight months, 17-year-old Diego Costa was soon left alone to cope with the daunting experience of his new life in Portugal with Sporting Braga. The telephone and internet became important allies in the fight against homesickness.

Although there was no language barrier, Costa did not take to the cold weather and unfamiliar cuisine in Portugal. The discipline demanded of young players also proved to be an obstacle and at times he was sorely tempted to give up. On one occasion he phoned his dad back in Lagarto to discuss his doubts but ended the call agreeing to fight on. "He promised not to give up. I think he didn't want to let me down," remembers Zeinha.

The then Penafiel coach, Rui Bento, a playing contemporary of Portugal's Golden Generation of Figo, Rui Costa and company, gave Costa his first break.

"A few of my former team-mates mentioned him to me so I went to watch him play," Bento told the Spanish paper *As*. "I could see that he was something special immediately, a rough diamond. I needed quality players at Penafiel, so I decided to take him."

Bento's friend, the football agent Nuno Patrao, explains: "In those days Mendes took everyone to Braga, but they didn't have a youth programme at the time and so the youngsters had to find an alternative."

Costa spent the first half of the 2006-2007 season in Penafiel, cutting his teeth in the rough and ready Portuguese second division, nicknamed the *Liga de Honra* (League of Honour). However, within weeks of his arrival, the youngster had already been spotted by representatives of the club which was to propel him into the highest levels of football: Atlético Madrid.

"I heard about Diego Costa from a few different sources," explains Jesús García Pitarch (Suso) the then director of football for *Los Colchoneros* (Atlético are nicknamed 'the Mattress-Makers'). "Jorge Mendes had brought us [Giourkas] Seitaridis, Maniche and Costinha and just before the start of the season he told me about a kid who had ended up in Braga and then on loan to Penafiel. It was Diego, of course. 'Take a look at him and tell me what you think,' Mendes told me.

"Later I was in another meeting and the technical secretary told me that they had heard good things about a Brazilian lad playing at Penafiel."

Javier Hernández, a scout for Atlético, was also alerted to the young player's raw talent. "I was at a match in Braga and at half-time we were enjoying the VIP buffet. I happened to overhear someone in the corridor chatting about some kid from Brazil who was 1.9m tall, just 17 and good with the ball. It was Nuno Patrao, who represented [Atlético defender] Zé Castro at the time, talking to Rui Bento. Nuno had actually brought me there to see Rolando, who was playing at Os Belenenses at the time, but he kept going on about this other boy. So I decided to go and watch him play in a Chaves-Penafiel game the next day and that's where I got my first sight of Diego Costa. It was a tiny stadium with just the one stand and very similar to the kind of football grounds you get in the third division in Spain. I wanted to go incognito, so I didn't ask for accreditation or team sheets. I just paid my money like everyone else. I remember the poor lad was knocked about all over the park that day by the older players who obviously saw him as some little kid. And he suffered all this as the lone striker which, for me, he shouldn't be. He's not a pure No.9, more of a second striker who needs to receive the ball, turn and run at goal."

Hernández talks about that first sighting of Costa as if it were yesterday. "I saw a technically gifted big lad who was still a bit uncoordinated. I could tell that he wasn't following any kind of healthy diet because he was a bit overweight. He obviously still needed a lot of work, but the boy was running all over the pitch, taking on all-comers with a kind of ferocity I had never seen before, bringing the ball down nicely, going one-on-one with defenders, looking to use the ball well, getting his head to it when necessary – I remember thinking, 'I can't believe this is a 17-year-old kid'. They were all going in hard on him and not once did he back down. Watching him that day I knew instinctively that this guy was special."

For his part, Rui Bento was convinced that Costa had potential and he made it his business to look after the youngster from the outset.

"Rui told me that the kid was a phenomenon," recalls Nuno Patrao. "Rui had worked with Cristiano Ronaldo and had also seen his debut. He told me that the young Brazilian reminded him of Ronaldo. He said the boy had it all. And Rui doesn't say that about just anybody."

Bento himself likes to tell the tale of the day he sent Costa, already physically out of the ordinary for a kid of his age, to a medical centre so that they could calibrate the physical potential of his quad muscles. According to Bento the specialist who examined this burgeoning

Brazilian was astonished at his physique. He had never seen anything like it.

Atlético's interest in the player was growing. "Julián Muñoz told me how good he was, despite the fact that he was still in the second division," says Nuno Patrao. "I remember the pair of us saw him training in torrential rain one day. We opted to stay in the car and watch from there! Then Jesús came to see him at a Varzim-Penafiel game."

García Pitarch takes up the story. "Julián Muñoz, the club's technical secretary, and I decided to go and see him play one Sunday morning. It had been raining all night and the pitch was so muddy they could hardly play the game. It was the first time I had set eyes on Costa in the flesh. There were a couple of Levante people there too and I remember both Julián and I were struck by his strength, his intense absorption in the game and the sheer grit he displayed, despite the fact that the pitch made running almost impossible. l went back to watch him a couple of times and then told Jorge Mendes that I wanted to meet the lad.

"So, it's all arranged and we meet met up at the Mendes' house in Oporto, all of us enjoying the lunch made by Sandra, Jorge's wife. The rest of us are chatting away but I can't get a word out of the boy. He sits there looking petulant whilst I explain that I've seen him play three times and talk him through what I like about his game and where we might go from here. I tell him that we'd like him to come to Atlético and he literally doesn't say a word, just sits there looking like he's in a massive sulk. I swear, we sat around Jorge's table for two hours and I couldn't get more than three words out of him. I was a bit taken aback and thought to myself, 'The lights are on but nobody's home'. Later, after a bit of reflection, I realised that I'd read him wrong. Diego was just an overgrown kid. He needed more experience and lots of playing time. He still had a lot of maturing to do. And that's completely normal. If you could have seen Kun Agüero when he started! Anyway, the club reassured us that his behaviour there was exemplary and that set my mind at rest."

Los Colchoneros decided to move fast. The name Diego Costa was bouncing around big clubs in Portugal. Javier Hernández recalls: "Jorge Mendes had his finger on the pulse there and he warned us that Oporto were also interested in the lad. But Suso was faster."

"My policy is – if you like a player, sign him fast," agrees García Pitarch. "You'll find out soon enough if you've made the right choice and if you delay, other clubs tend to get interested and things become complicated. So we signed him and almost immediately a few other clubs did express an interest.

"Within a week Eugenio Botas, a Recreativo scout, called me up and said, 'Suso, I've just come all the way to Portugal to sign a player up and they tell me that Atlético has already got him. I've told them that

that's impossible. Why on earth would you sign Diego Costa?'

"'Because he's a good player of course.'

"'Well, we've had our eye on him for a while and want to sign him. Maybe we could come to some arrangement?'

"So I told him straight, 'Costa is an Atlético Madrid player now and that's final'. We had reacted with more speed than everyone else and by the time they all began to show an interest, he was already signed up.

"The deal gave us 50% of his rights, leaving Braga with the other 50%. Mendes had told me from the word go that Braga wouldn't sell the player outright and that was fine with me. So, by October or November we had paid €1.5m for a guy who had played three games in the Portuguese second division. Even if they had been able to buy him outright, Recreativo or any other team wouldn't have paid more than €200,000 for him. Looking back, it was a bit reckless and a few people thought we were mad at the time, but we were convinced. We really rated him. For some, his physical strength was the draw, for others his youthful energy, but all of us recognised his sheer talent."

Now that Atlético owned 50% of the player, the priority was to rescue him from the *Liga de Honra*, where he had already scored five goals.

"When we made the deal we agreed that he was too good to play at Penafiel. We decided he should go back to Braga so he could play in the first division," explains García Pitarch. "So they took him back in January."

The then Braga goalkeeper, Dani Mallo, initially wasn't over impressed by the new recruit. "At the start he didn't really stand out that much from all the other Brazilian kids who came to play in Portugal. He adapted pretty quickly because we had quite a few Brazilian players at the time and they looked after him. Maciel, Vandinho and Wender, who were his best mates, called him *Miúdo*, which means 'the Kid' in Portuguese. He was actually pretty full of himself from the start. Almost too confident. Always blasting out his music. I remember him taking the piss out of me when he'd been there for about four days. And I was 10 years his senior! One of our most experienced players at the time was João Pinto. He was hugely respected and many of us were a bit in awe of him. And would you believe it? Costa even had a go at him!

"The kid really made his presence felt on the pitch, too. He wasn't as strong back then, but he went in hard for every tackle. He'd kick the shit out of you but, in fairness, was also happy to take it if you responded in kind. That's what made me sit up and take notice. Apart from the guys playing up front for Oporto and Benfica, the rest of the strikers in the Portuguese league at the time were pretty soft. I remember thinking that he would struggle at Atlético. His size and strength made him seem more of an enforcer than a pure goalscorer.

A stick-out memory from then was when we played at Beira Mar and lost 1-0 in a game where he had a one-on-one chance to tuck away the equaliser but he couldn't beat the keeper. Now though? God only knows what his limits are.

"Life in Braga is pretty slow. People are very religious and there are more than 300 churches in the city," Mallo continues. "But the press are very critical and outspoken and the president at the time, Antonio Salvador, was obsessed with football. He even sat on the bench for our first 10 games, something I'd never seen happen anywhere else.

"The coach, Rogério Gonçalves, was very demanding and had no patience at all. Then Jorge Costa came and things got better. Strategically he was very like Mourinho and he was the kind of guy who looked after his players. His assistant was Aloísio, an ex-Barça player, who was a fantastic guy. We had a good season that year and ended up qualifying for the Europa League."

It was in this competition that Diego Costa would score his only goal for the *Guerreiros do Minho*.

Braga played Parma away on February 22, 2007, in the last 16. Costa came on for Zé Carlos in the 71st minute with the score at 0-0 and took just 20 frantic minutes to earn a booking and then convert the winning goal in the last minute. As the game approached added time, he banged home a volley from Filipe's cross and sealed the team's progress into the quarter-finals.

However, just as the player was beginning to make his name at the club, things took a turn for the worse. García Pitarch explains: "Diego was very unlucky and fractured his metatarsal after just seven games. Back then players with that kind of injury were still allowed to play games but were told not to train. He told me on the phone that he wasn't training, so we brought him [to Spain] so that Doctor Villalón could have a look at him, and he decided that he needed an operation. He ended up being out for nearly six months and only got back to playing in August."

The injury marked the end of Costa's Portuguese sojourn, as Spanish football beckoned.

"My recommendation was to start him out in Atléti's youth team in Segunda B so that he could mature a bit," explains Javier Hernández. "He needed to put on a bit more muscle, improve his diet and learn our tactical systems. But Suso was more ambitious and decided to loan him out immediately."

Costa arrived at Barajas airport a complete nobody. "No-one recognised him when we picked him up at the airport," says Javier Fernández. "Nowadays he can't even walk down the street! I remember it was pretty chilly that day but Pedro Pablo Matesanz, who picked him up, told us that the boy had arrived in Bermuda shorts and flip-flops! That's how he started his life in Spain."

"There are two or three players that I'm particularly

proud of having signed in my life," García Pitarch tells me. "Sissoko, who I bought from the Auxerre youth team for €190,000, Miranda, Ricardo Oliveira and, of course, Diego Costa. Although obviously I take no credit for Diego's success. Everything he has achieved he has done himself."

So far, his achievements were little more than a brief tour of duty in the League of Honour and an unfortunate cameo with Braga, the team who retained half of his rights as he made his move to Spain.

3

CELTA VIGO: THE GOOD, THE BAD AND THE UGLY

'Therefore, just as water retains no constant shape, so in warfare there are no constant conditions'

Sun Tzu, *The Art of War*

IT WAS SETTLED – upon his arrival in Spain, Diego Costa would not play for Atlético B. Instead, his parent club would seek a loan move to develop his raw talent. "This guy had real talent and I wanted him competing immediately," explains Jesús García Pitarch, then Atlético's director of football. "I wanted to see him playing matches and improving his game. I was one of the people who insisted that he leave Portugal. Their second division is very poor and there are really only three seriously competitive teams in their first division. When those teams play each other you get a bit of quality but otherwise, teams like Olhanense or Estoril are just a joke. He would have a much better chance of improving his game in Spain. I wanted him here as soon as possible, adapting to our way of life, learning the language and starting the process of applying for Spanish nationality."

Costa was sent to the club's summer training camp, just another young player honing his football skills. For Costa though, this would be the first of many summers sweating in the *rojiblanca* jersey.

His presentation to the media on July 10, 2007 was memorable for two reasons. Firstly, president Enrique Cerezo boldly declared that they had signed "the new Kaká" and the club took the unusual step of providing the media, who at that time knew little or nothing about the player, with a surprise extra in the official press pack. Journalist Sergio Perela, who was at the event, explains: "He was such an unknown that as well as the usual press pack, they gave us a DVD showing some footage of him playing."

That morning, speaking in a Portuguese not dissimilar to the Spanish he speaks today, Costa described himself as a "second striker, with a good burst of pace" and assured the packed VIP suite in the Vicente Calderón that he had always dreamed of "playing for a great club like this" and hoped to prove to them "just what I'm made of".

Atlético's pre-season had kicked off the day before the press conference, on July 9, when they played Manzanares FC. Ahead lay the qualifying ties of the Intertoto Cup, which would be their ticket into the UEFA Cup. It would prove a bumpy ride. A solitary goal from Atlético's Diego Forlán in the second leg reversed a 2-1 loss to Gloria Bistrita in Romania on away goals. Costa, however, took no part in these early stages of Atlético's European campaign.

"Costa had just come back from his injury and he

used to come to training with his laces undone," reflects García Pitarch on the Brazilian's early days in Spain. "He also tended to be at the back of the pack whenever the squad was doing laps and clearly preferred to stick to the inside lane, where you end up covering a shorter distance. The first team coach, Javier Aguirre, came to see me one day and had a bit of a moan. 'That lad's a real pain in the arse and the sooner you loan him out and get him out of my hair, the better. He's a disaster who runs around with his shoelaces undone.'

"I'm afraid I was a bit short with him. I said, 'Javier, that's what you're here for – to teach him how to do things right. I bet it hasn't even occurred to you that he keeps his shoelaces undone because he's just come back from a six-month injury and he's still in pain. And maybe he takes the inside lane because he doesn't know any better. It's your job to educate the lad and explain this stuff to him. Don't just assume he knows what he should be doing. We're not talking about a 30-year-old pro here. This is an 18-year-old kid who is still learning.'

"Then two weeks later Javier comes back to me and says, 'You were right. I had a chat with him and he's taken it all on board. I'm delighted'.

"Sometimes you have to give young players a bit of extra help to stop them messing up."

Costa also failed to feature in the pre-season tournament which took place in Amsterdam in August that year. Atlético were defeated in the semi-finals by an Ajax side which included Klaas-Jan Huntelaar and Wesley Sneijder, but then won the consolation match against Lazio.

He had to wait until August 11, 2007 and the *Ciudad de Vigo* tournament to make his debut. *Los Colchoneros* eventually won the game against Celta de Vigo in a penalty shoot-out after having missed two spot-kicks in the first half. A rather ungainly looking Costa came on after the break for the recently signed Simão Sabrosa to face the players that, unknown to him, would shortly become his team-mates.

García Pitarch: "We played a friendly against Celta de Vigo and we were talking to their sports director Ramón Martínez about loaning him some players. He had called us to ask for Mario Suárez, but in the end he also took Costa."

"There had been a general exodus after our relegation and we were in dire need of some new blood," remembers Martínez. "Costa played for 45 minutes in the *Ciudad de Vigo* and although he didn't do a great deal, you could see how confident he was. Then we saw him play against Getafe about 10 days later where he had an excellent 45 minutes. You could see he had something about him. I had put out feelers about him but after that match I was pretty sure we wanted him."

Aguirre had decided to rest his top players and save them for the UEFA Cup games (by this stage Atlético had already played away in the first round to Vojvodina of Serbia) thereby giving Michael Laudrup's Getafe the chance to dominate a weaker Atlético side. In the 55th minute, the Mexican coach replaced José Manuel Jurado with Costa. This was the opportunity the Brazilian had been waiting for and in the 71st minute he opened the scoring. A great pass from José Antonio Reyes over the top of the Getafe defence was killed by Costa and then thumped at goal off his right foot. Though Roberto Abbondanzieri got his gloves to it, the shot was so fierce that it bent his wrists back and the ball went in. Costa's first goal on Spanish soil was shortly followed by his first yellow card, and a pattern was set for the years ahead.

His performance had been enough to convince the Celta directors who believed he could play a key role in their campaign to return to *La Liga*.

"We all got together in the Goizeko restaurant in Madrid's Wellington Hotel – Ramón Martínez, Manuel García Quilón, Miguel Ángel Gil Marín and I," recalls Jesús García Pitarch. "And we agreed to loan them Mario Suárez and Diego Costa. I told Ramón straight out that they would need to keep on top of Diego because he still needed to learn how to behave like a professional. He had practically no club experience and didn't really understand the code of conduct we expect in the dressing room. He was pretty much an *ingénue* in all of that. 'If you leave him to his own devices it will be a disaster. It'll cost you financially and deprive me of a potentially great player,' I told him."

Costa was still an unknown quantity when he arrived at Vigo. "I had just come back from injury and people were perhaps not expecting a lot from me," he says.

Roberto Lago, who had just broken into the Celta first team, agrees. "None of us had heard of him when he arrived and we were all pretty surprised when he turned out to be such a good player."

Ramón Martínez: "We were delighted with his football from day one. That was when we started to believe that we had the squad we needed to move up."

Unfortunately Celta's high hopes would, in the end, be dashed. Several of the squad which had crashed out of the *Primera* the previous season had remained with the club, including manager Hristo Stoichkov, who had been rushed in to replace the unfortunate Fernando Vázquez towards the end of the disastrous 2006/7 campaign. Costa's game has since been compared to that of the feisty Stoichkov in his pomp, and he soon became a regular in the teams selected by the former Ballon d'Or winner. The Brazilian, in white boots and rolled down socks over shin guards cut down especially by the Celta kit men, was soon scoring goals for his new side. He also quickly became the centre of attention for other, less laudable reasons.

In their seventh league match, Celta played Xerez at home and were dominating the match. Costa got his first goal in *La Liga*, diving in to the six-yard box to finish with 15 minutes left. He raised his hands to the sky in a gesture that spoke as much of sheer relief as any religious devotion. But his celebration did not end there. His Celta team-mate Jesús Perera described it: "I remember he went to the corner and started fooling around with the ball, prancing about like a bull fighter."

The Xerez players were quick to react and Costa, never one to back down from a confrontation, responded by laughing at them. All hell broke loose.

Agus, a Celta defender that day, recalls: "Antoñito [a striker for Xerez] in particular took it badly but Brazilians can be like that and I don't think he really intended to offend anyone."

"He didn't play in the corresponding game at Xerez," adds Fernando Sales, then of Celta. "It was just as well because no-one there had forgotten him. We did explain to him after the match that you can't behave like that in Spain."

The referee showed Costa a yellow card, his second of the match, and his first sending off since arriving in Spain.

He apologised at the press conference later. "I messed up and I'm sorry. I know I shouldn't have done it, but it was just a spur of the moment thing. It won't happen again."

When asked about rumours of more trouble in the tunnel after the match, Costa denied involvement in any incident but confirmed that, had anything happened, he most certainly would have been a part of it. "Nothing happened afterwards. You know, I'm no coward. I'm a man and I'm not scared of anything."

His public apology did not save him from his manager's rebuke. "Stoichkov went absolutely apeshit," remembers team-mate Antonio Núñez.

Within days the Bulgarian had decided to go, citing personal reasons. "I was waiting for a good result before I made the decision to leave," explained Stoichkov. The news came as less of a surprise to everyone inside the club, where it was an open secret that assistant coach Antonio López had been taking all strategic and tactical decisions. Hristo packed his bags and was replaced by Juan Ramón López Caro.

Meanwhile, Costa was faced with the challenge of adapting to life in a new city whilst maintaining a strong performance on the pitch. His main ally in this was Eugenio González, known as 'Bosman' at the club because of his role in settling in foreign players. "We got on like a house on fire from the start and I was happy to help him find a place of his own," recalls González. "I remember how passionate he was about football. Training wasn't enough for him and he used to play with his mates on the university pitches at 11pm. I said to him, 'Diego, you can't keep doing that. You're going to do yourself an injury'. But he couldn't help himself. Football was his life and he was either playing it himself or watching the Brazilian league on television."

As it turned out, Bosman was wrong and the young Brazilian continued to enjoy his late night sorties under the Gallegan stars with no ill effect. Meanwhile, his game was winning Costa legions of fans. "Diego Costa, the new Celta sensation is more than ready for Sporting," declared the *Faro de Vigo* newspaper before a visit to Real Sporting, which ended with him scoring the winning goal.

Costa's time in the second division was characterised both by the strong performances so popular with the fans and the mis-steps which betrayed his inexperience: "It's true, sometimes I get confused and keep dribbling when I should really be going for a goal," he confessed.

Regardless of his rough edges, Spanish football was witnessing the emergence of a star in the making. Commentators began to draw comparisons with the Egyptian player Mido, another gifted yet volatile striker. "I need to talk less and work harder," was Costa's own comment.

His new coach, López Caro, was quick to see Costa's potential but also had to endure the player's idiosyncratic behaviour.

During their 16th league game, against Seville Atlético, the young Brazilian was booked first for diving and then, 19 minutes later, for his almost continual protests at the referee's decisions. Down to 10 men, Celta fought back from a goal down to draw, but the atmosphere in the Balaídos stadium had shifted. The fans who had applauded him as he left the pitch after his first red card were now murmuring in disapproval.

Costa's appearances were frequently marred by disputes. The previous week, away at Malaga, the Brazilian kneed the defender Weligton in the head, causing an injury which required six stitches. After the match, the Malaga player revealed that this had not been his first experience of Costa, whom he had encountered in his League of Honour days with Penafiel and warned referees that they should keep an eye on the player. Costa responded in no uncertain terms: "I wasn't out to injure him but he was kicking me, Contreras and Quincy all over the pitch the whole game. He and their goalie were way over the top in their tackles on me but, just because I didn't end up bleeding, no-one's talking about that. I don't need to hit people in order to play good football. I'm not a boxer after all. But Weligton is happy to throw a few punches himself. It's just that he's dishonest about it. I don't know what he's sniveling about anyway. He's such a big girl. Maybe he should take up volleyball instead."

The next day the Malaga press led with: 'Diego Costa raises hell in the second division.'

In all likelihood the striker was more irritated by the hard tackles on the Dutchman Quincy Owusu-Abeyie, who was his best friend at the time. "They were always together," recalls Antonio Núñez. "The rest of us couldn't understand how they communicated, because one of them could only speak Portuguese and the other stuck to English all the time."

Team-mate Roberto Lago explains: "Diego told me how they did it: 'I don't speak English so we use sign language instead.' We were actually worried that he would be led astray by Quincy, who was a bit of a rebel." Ramón Martínez echoes this sentiment: "Quincy was a phenomenal player but totally unmanageable."

By the time the winter break arrived, Celta seemed to have turned the corner. Before he left for the holidays, Costa told the press: "I promise there will be no more bad behaviour once I'm back from Brazil." The start of the second half of the season brought unwelcome news however, when López Caro decided to leave him off the team sheet for a couple of games in favour of the Cypriot Ioannis Okkas. This decision was interpreted as a punishment. Although Costa was seen as a versatile player – he had been used on either wing as well as through the middle – the coach was unhappy with his lack of intensity in training sessions. It was not until March 23 that he would produce the kind of performance that would come to characterise his early career.

A few days before, the club had sacked Juan Ramón López Caro. President Carlos Mouriño, having sounded out his advisors and sports director, decided that, with the team still nine points behind the top spots, a fresh approach was urgently required. "[López Caro] was the one who understood Diego the best," says Lago. "He really tried to bring him along, get the best out of him," says Esteban, the goalkeeper of that Celta team.

With interim coach, Antonio López in charge, Costa returned for an away game against Numancia on the frozen pitch of Los Pajaritos stadium, after spending two weeks on the bench. "I had told López in no uncertain terms, 'Antonio, you've spent the last year telling me that this boy's a *crack* [top quality player] and how much you rate his football and yet now that you're in charge, you're not even giving him a game'," Jesús García Pitarch recalls.

With the Canal Plus cameras trained on the pitch, Costa trotted on to replace Ariel Rosada with his team a goal down. The Brazilian not only led the comeback against Numancia but almost singlehandedly turned the whole match around. Diego Costa had come into his own.

Forty-three seconds after he took to the pitch, José Jesús Perera made a break down the left, fed Costa and the striker reached the penalty area before side-footing the ball between the legs of the goalkeeper, Jacobo.

Then, within a few minutes, Costa converted one of the most spectacular goals in Spanish football that year. "I remember that we stole the ball and then I ended up feeding Diego the pass which produced the key move of the game," says Antonio Núñez.

Celta were penned in at the back as Numancia

pushed for the winner. Núñez fed Costa the ball, he turned and, although he was still in his own half, headed for goal. Off he went on a crazy slalom, past one, past two, a change of pace and then the ball crashed in off the laces of his boot.

Adolfo Barbero, who was commentating, exploded: "An incredible goal from Diego Costa! Absolutely amazing!"

"The minute I got the ball I looked up and thought, 'I have to go for it'," recalls Costa. "So when I reached the area I took aim and fired. Luckily for me everything worked and I scored. I love it when I finish like that."

With his arms extended Costa sprinted over to the Celta fans, pointing to his jersey. "It was definitely one of the best goals of my career, but my career isn't over yet," he said post-match.

Two goals and an unforgettable win over the league leaders. "Whenever I go back to Numancia I remember that goal. It was pure Diego," says Agus, another team-mate that day.

Antonio López's appointment did not bring the kind of immediate success the club were looking for and after only nine games in charge the coach resigned. "The reason for López's departure is his failure to manage and direct the first team players," read a terse statement.

"We were no longer fighting for promotion. We were fighting to avoid relegation," is how Fernando Sales puts it.

The Celta board found their fourth coach of the season in their own youth system in the shape of Alejandro Menéndez, who recalls: "The team had become very negative and the players' confidence had really dipped. People had begun to think the worst. Luckily though, in the third part of the season, we started to turn things around and managed to survive."

Menéndez did not use Costa much, preferring instead to put the team's fate in the hands of more experienced players. In the one match Costa did start, the striker earned his third sending off of the season. His reaction afterwards took the coach aback. Menéndez takes up the story: "We were playing Tenerife in Balaídos and were winning 2-0 in the 20th minute, by which time he had already got himself a yellow card. Then, as we tried to take a quick free-kick, Costa hauled an opponent away from the ball, got a second yellow and left us with 10 men. We ended up with a 2-2 draw and in the dressing room after the game he came up to me and with that almost childlike frankness of his said, '*Mister,* please forgive me. I'm still young and I know I have a lot to learn'.

"I was surprised and impressed that a player had the guts and honesty to recognise that he had messed up and damaged the team's chances. It was the same with training. If he turned up late, he wouldn't give you a load of bullshit. There would be none of the usual, 'the alarm didn't go off' rubbish. He would be totally upfront and tell me he'd been up most of the night playing PlayStation. It made me really warm to him."

Costa also apologised to the public: "This has taught me a hard lesson. I have to learn from it. I have to change. I have no idea why these things keep happening to me," he said, his head bowed.

Celta finished the season having saved themselves by the skin of their teeth, not much recompense for a team which had started the season with high hopes. "People ended up not thinking much of me. They saw me as a bit of a trouble maker," reflected Costa. "It's important to change people's impressions. I always commit myself to the teams I play for and always want to win. I hate losing. It's just that at times I go about things the wrong way and that created problems."

His relationship with the fans had been bittersweet. Despite the fact that he and the Uruguayan Canobbio were almost unanimously seen as the two best players in the squad, the fans disliked what they saw as his constant dissent on the pitch and his tendency to want too much time on the ball.

"He could lose it too easily back then, although in some of those games the referees and opposition players were kind of waiting to see if they could provoke him," says Antonio Núñez.

"It was clear he was headed for bigger things," adds Agus. "You could see in him things that most players don't have. I loved how he played with his back to goal, held it up against even the toughest defence and then turned to run at goal with such ease. And he didn't care who he went up against – whether it was an older, more experienced player or not. There are some strikers who back down if you give them a bit of a shove, but not him. He would keep coming no matter how much you kicked him. His development has been very similar to that of Álvaro Negredo, whom I've also played with. They have both worked to perfect their game and are now brilliant strikers."

"He had almost everything you need to make a great forward," Esteban adds. "You could see how talented he was back then, although he wasn't as good as he is now. He was brilliant up front and what really struck me was how well he played under pressure."

"Of his armoury of skills perhaps, back then, it was his finishing he had to work on most," adds Canobbio.

"Of all the players I've worked with he's the one who can get away from three players in the tightest of spaces without any need to look particularly elegant doing it," explains Roberto Lago. "There were games when he was out of sight. And he was amazing in training."

His Celta team-mates are unanimous about Costa the man. Super-competitive and nasty on the park, off it he was the opposite. After overcoming initial shyness and the language barrier, the striker became a larger-than-life presence around the club. "He always arrived in his car with the music at full volume," says Agus.

"Always singing and dancing," adds Fernando Sales.

At one of his last press conferences, Costa expressed his love for the club and the city, and his desire to stay. But Celta were fighting insolvency and in negotiations with their creditors. "Celta let him go and ended up not paying him because they had to make their creditors the priority. He was really pissed off about it," recalls García Pitarch. "Of course Atlético then had to pay him all the money he was owed."

Looking back at those early years, Costa said: "I grew up thinking a bit of pushing and shoving was completely normal. Then I suddenly learned that if you kick another player, you get in trouble. Nobody had ever reprimanded me for that before."

"He needed a guiding hand," says García Pitarch. "You had to try to understand some of the stuff he did, and show him a bit of patience. Above all, we needed to educate him."

4

ALBACETE: A CITY WITHOUT A BEACH

'He whom the ancients called an intelligent warrior is one who not only wins but who excels at winning with ease'

Sun Tzu, *The Art of War*

"DO YOU HAVE any idea who we're signing? Only the guy who's going to keep us up." Albacete coach Juan Ignacio Martínez spoke bullishly as he locked horns with the club's vice president of football, Gonzalo Panadero.

"Listen, when this guy arrives, I'm going to have to recruit two psychologists – one for him and one for you," Panadero retorted.

With the end of July 2008 approaching, Albacete were still desperately looking for one more player for their squad but not everyone agreed that Diego Costa was the best man for the job. Stories of the young Brazilian's wayward behaviour had spread far and wide, blackening his name forever in some quarters. However, the plans for his transfer to Albacete had been laid down weeks before, in the face of interest from rival clubs Nàstic and Salamanca. The player had his own ideas about the destination for his next loan move, but they were quickly quashed.

"Diego phoned me up out of the blue to tell me that Málaga's coach, Juan Muñiz, was interested in him," recalls Jesús García Pitarch, then Atlético's director of football. "I told him that Málaga was out of the question. All I could think of was that boy let loose on the Costa del Sol. The people at Vigo had kept me informed about the things that had happened whilst he was there and there was no way I would consider Málaga. In fact, I was already thinking about Albacete. Diego wasn't keen at first but we managed to convince him in the end."

Antonio Alfaro, an agent with close ties to Albacete, was so impressed by Costa in a pre-season friendly between Atlético and Getafe that he immediately contacted García Pitarch to try and broker a move.

At this point, the Brazilian had played a few friendlies for Atlético and had even travelled with them on a tour of Mexico, but had not yet secured a regular place in the first team. Albacete, on the other hand, were in urgent need of a strong player up front.

"Antonio told me that they needed a forward but that they couldn't pay for him," continues García Pitarch. "I wasn't particularly bothered about the money and just wanted him to play, so in the end we drew up a contract which meant that the more games he played, the less they paid. Basically it would end up costing them if they didn't let him play."

The Albacete coach, Martínez, already knew the player. While in charge at Salamanca the year before he had faced Costa, then on loan at Celta Vigo. "He basically made mincemeat out of my guys, so when Alfaro told me that he was available I told him to get down to Madrid immediately and sign him up," says Martínez.

Costa signed his contract on August 22, 2008, and three days later was presented as Albacete's new striker. Flanked by director of football Máximo Hernández and president Ubaldo González, a relaxed and smiling Costa – wearing a grey t-shirt and a black baseball cap, back to front – was perhaps overly optimistic that day. "I am determined to play in the first division and am happy to prove myself here in the second division. I will be working hard to help Albacete win promotion."

"Diego was labouring under a couple of serious misconceptions when he arrived," grins Martínez. "First of all, he had no idea that Albacete wasn't on the coast and therefore didn't have a beach and, secondly, he thought he was coming to a much better team. The first game he saw us play was the final of the Castilla La Mancha Cup in Puertollano. He attended the match but didn't play because he hadn't yet met all his team-mates. I made a point of being completely up front with him about the quality of the players we had and at half-time he told me that, after having seen the kind of football we were producing, there was no way he was staying. He was adamant. He was going back to Madrid!"

Albacete midfielder Marco Navas remembers Costa telling him shortly after his arrival that his agent had sent him to Albacete. "You could tell that he had absolutely no idea where he was."

The Brazilian scored Albacete's first goal of the season, a winner in the final moments of their first match, against Sevilla's B team.

The club's new striker would also become a central figure in the Carlos Belmonte stadium dressing room. "Definitely one of the best group of lads I've ever played with," remembers defender Francisco Javier Tarantino. "Thursday was the hardest day of training so every Thursday and sometimes on a Monday, we'd all head over to Diego's flat."

The player had a huge terrace and would invite his team-mates over for post-training barbecues. "Although only if Diego Trotta was there," qualifies Marco Navas. The Argentine defender was the only one who knew how to cook.

Poker games would frequently drift on until 1am and Costa, who lived alone, had people coming and going at all hours of the day and night. It was inevitable that his nocturnal habits would raise issues. One night in particular the police turned up after Costa's neighbour had complained about the smell from the barbecue. "They lined us all up and demanded to see identification and then gave us a good talking to," says Trotta, the Argentine defender. "Of course the meat had been cooking all this time and by the time they had finished, it was cooked to perfection."

Costa's unfortunate neighbour may have been one of the few Albacete citizens who did not appreciate the new-found togetherness in the dressing room of his hometown team.

Vicente Ferre de la Rosa, an administrator at the club, was the recipient of many of her calls. "On one occasion they had a porn movie blaring out and the poor woman came down to tell them to turn the volume down. 'What's the matter? Don't you like making love?' a wide-eyed Costa asked her sweetly."

In the end, she followed Costa's trail back to Madrid and complained directly to Jesús García Pitarch at Atléti about the menace he had sent to Albacete. "She said that every time she banged on the wall to get them to turn down the music, they just played it even louder," he remembers.

Whilst living in Albacete, Costa also bought a dog. The big, aggressive striker did not opt for the pit bull or Rottweiler, which might have best suited his playing style. No, Costa's dog was a Yorkshire Terrier. "I had a dog as well and we used to have a real laugh with them," remembers Marco Navas. "Although mine was bigger, he was really scared of Diego's. That thing might have been small, but my God, it was fierce – not unlike its owner."

As the Thursday night poker club continued, Costa became almost as skilled in the game as he was with a ball. Trotta, his tutor in this new discipline, taught him well, and soon he was a regular winner at the table. The poker-playing team-mates chanced their luck in more ways than one. "We even took part in the European Poker Tour in Madrid. We told them that we were professional players from Brazil and Argentina. What a blast!" remembers Trotta.

Even the coach ended up facing Costa's impenetrable poker face. Costa, donning his poker uniform of a baseball cap, sunglasses and a vest top, sometimes convinced Juan Ignacio Martínez to join in the fun. "They'd usually fleece me, the bastards."

Although Costa's talent for poker was proving a steady source of income, the same could not be said for his wages. In fact, such were the club's financial difficulties that they were unable to cover the wage bill on more than one occasion during his loan spell.

The club's medical assistant, Manolo Bleda, remembers: "The club decided to pay the players but not the rest of the staff. When he heard that, Diego refused to train until everyone was paid. In 35 years I have never known anyone else take a stand like that."

"He always checked with the kit men to see if they had been paid," continues Eduardo Rodríguez Vellando, the club doctor. "And he would give his team-mates a hard time if he heard them grumbling whilst other members of staff hadn't even been paid. Then one day the president came into the dressing room. He was going round everyone shaking their hands. Diego waited for his turn, and then kept his hands by his side and asked if the kit men had been paid. 'I'm not shaking your hand until you pay them,' he said."

The team performed moderately well, with Costa playing a key role in every match. He didn't miss a league game until December 13, when Albacete played Real Sociedad at home. Martínez explains: "There had been a huge bust up between him and Jonathan, our goalkeeper. I remember it was over something really trivial – one of them had asked for the ball and the other didn't get it to him fast enough. We were playing Real Sociedad at home next and since I felt I had to be fair about it, I made both of them substitutes. It was absolutely freezing and he was sitting there wrapped up in his big jacket, looking miserable. I turned to my assistant, Javi Pereira, and told him to put Diego on at half-time. He hardly warmed up, just sprinted out onto the pitch and, in the 93rd minute, scored the winning goal."

The two warring players cleared the air the next day at training and sealed the deal with a brotherly hug in the middle of the training pitch. "He was totally sincere about it and even said that, if we were sick of him and wanted him out, he'd go," remembers team-mate Carlos Merino.

The transformation between the all-in competitor and the nice guy could be instant, and subject to the strangest triggers. During a game against Nàstic, a lung-bursting run from Costa was ended by a foul inside the box. He demanded to take the penalty, and found opposition from Verza, his team-mate. Costa would not give an inch – until Verza explained that it was his birthday, at which point he happily stood down.

During training one day, Martínez decided to up the intensity and demanded more pressing from his players during a drill. Costa threw up his hands and announced he could not take any more, and stalked off to sit in the stands, sulking. His team-mates laughed it off at first, until eventually Trotta, who held the most influence over the Brazilian, was sent to talk him down. "He was just a big kid really," says Ferre de la Rosa, affectionately.

Jesús Cabrero tells an even better tale: "We were on the bus coming back from a Real Sociedad game in San Sebastián and we stopped at a service station at about 2am. We got out for a while and when we got back to the bus we found two guys nicking our stuff. Diego just went for them. What a sight! The two guys sprinting away across a field with Diego hot on their heels, screaming and swearing at them in Portuguese and the rest of us chasing him trying to get him back. He was like a mad man."

On the pitch and in training, Costa's overwhelming competitive nature was being honed, but it was matched by a much subtler instinct for popping up in the right areas. "What surprised me was that every time there was a loose ball in an attacking situation it would seem to rebound to him," recalls team-mate Diego Mainz.

"Always. The first time can be pure luck but when it happens a third, fourth, fifth time you learn that it's not luck. It's him."

On matchday, Costa was already struggling with the reputation he had earned during his tempestuous loan at Celta Vigo. Martínez certainly felt that his striker was still paying for past crimes, but at the same time he could frequently empathise with match officials who had to provide boundaries for Costa. "Whenever I was refereeing in training and had to admonish him for something, I always avoided looking at him. It was better to just ignore his response. He'd go absolutely nuts." In one press conference, the coach conceded that Costa was great for 89 minutes, but that for one minute every match, it was better to avoid him.

Not that his frequent over-reactions were without provocation. Whenever the team was under pressure, they would simply thump the ball long to Costa who would expertly hold it up, but his physical presence at the spearhead of the Albacete attack came at a price.

"In those days in the *Segunda*, players were allowed to kick him black and blue," Bleda confirms. "I'd see his ankles sticking out of the stretcher as they carried him off."

Costa thrived on conflict and was not averse to deliberately provoking opposition defenders. Inevitably, it was a tactic which invited trouble. One such incident happened in the Heliodoro Rodríguez López stadium against Tenerife. Costa earned his second yellow minutes from the end of the match and began to protest, taking the name of the referee Hevia Obras' mother in vain. Obras formally recorded what happened next in his report.

"The No.19 [Costa] stopped and started to take off his shin guards instead of leaving the pitch. In response, Tenerife's No.5 [Manolo Martínez] asked him to get off the pitch. The No.19 responded aggressively and was issued with another warning. The confrontation then escalated into a brawl involving more players from both sides."

Martínez was aware of the balance that had to be struck between this raw talent and the volcanic temper that had the potential to derail it. He would frequently emphasise to the Brazilian the sheer scale of his talent and how far he could expect to go in the game. "But I also tried to make him understand that his reputation could damage him and that he had to change people's view of him," he says.

Off the pitch, Costa was fun-loving and care-free. He had become the team's DJ, and his team-mates found themselves learning the Brazilian songs they were being force-fed. The kitmen would walk into the dressing room to find their laundry basket upturned and being used as a drum by the young striker. He purchased speakers which he plugged into his mobile phone during the team's trips for away games, blaring his music at record-breaking volume. When his coach told him to dial it down, he responded: "We need it loud, boss – it will help us win."

It was midwinter and Costa's team-mate, Jaime Romero, himself just a youngster at the time, drove his brand new BMW to training, a present from his father for passing his driving test. By the time Romero trotted out of the dressing room, he found his beloved motor parked in the centre of the pitch beside a snowman, wrapped in toilet paper, all the doors wide open and with a madman behind the wheel, shouting and thumping the horn. Costa, of course. The whole thing was filmed by Martínez and the coach was often a silent partner in these pranks, which he would play back to his team in the hope of cementing the bond between them.

Costa was entranced when the first snow fell that winter. "One day we arrived at training and the whole pitch was white. Diego went crazy. He dived into it and started rolling about and then spent the whole training session throwing snowballs at the rest of us," recalls team-mate Tarantino.

During stays in hotels for away matches, Costa would place a pillow case over his head and 'kidnap' the unsuspecting club doctor. On another occasion, he apparently vanished during a training session. The hunt for the striker ended only when Costa emerged from his position, submerged in a pile of cut grass behind a lawnmower. If the Jacuzzi was overflowing with foam from an emptied bottle of shower gel, or if members of the coaching staff found themselves suddenly locked inside the sauna, the culprit was always the same. Verza, his team-mate, recalls that by now Costa was known merely as "that fucking Brazilian".

Romero's car was not the only one endangered by Costa. Martínez recalls his young striker rolling up in an Audi Q7, telling his team-mates that he was driving on his Brazilian licence. When the coach saw Costa lose control and go into a spin on the little roundabout at the entrance to the stadium, he asked Trotta to persuade his friend to take lessons.

On at least one occasion another team-mate was called upon to drive the Audi. Alberto Aguilar smiles as he recalls: "It was a home game and I was injured. Diego had his cousin and girlfriend staying with him but they were leaving that day, in the morning before the game, and he had promised to drive them to the airport. The boss came to me and said that since he couldn't be dissuaded from taking them, he wanted me to drive them. And I wasn't exactly an ace driver in those days. So I went to pick them up at the appointed hour and, of course, the little shit was late. Eventually he rushed out and said to me, 'Drive like the clappers. If you get a fine, I'll pay it'. I risked life and limb that day, but we made it to the airport on time *and* we won the game. What a day!"

The team, fighting hard to avoid relegation, had their fair share of setbacks but managed to stay away from the foot of the table. Despite this, tension was rife in the boardroom, where the directors were divided into two factions and things came to a head at the end of April, after a draw against Córdoba at home. To the team's horror, the board reacted to the poor result by sacking Martínez.

"When I said goodbye I tried to reassure them," says Martínez. "I told them not to worry. Even if they lost every game from then to the end of the season, they wouldn't go down unless Alavés won every game they played."

"The directors were inexperienced and they just got a bit spooked," explains Máximo Hernández, who as director of football had to take over coaching himself. "One minute they had kicked Juan Ignacio out and the next they were telling me that they had no money for another coach and I'd have to do it."

None of the players could understand the decision. Costa who, in Verza's words, was "the *Mister's* right-hand man" was furious.

"I had to calm him down because he was threatening to leave too," recalls Antonio Alfaro, the agent who had first connected Albacete with Costa and retained an influence on the volatile striker. "I sat him down and said to him, 'I'm speaking to you man to man now and you might not like it. God has given you a supernatural talent and you can't waste it. God has sent you here to play football. I know you care about your friend but you can't do this'. In the end he accepted what I was saying."

Alfaro had developed a conceptual three-second rule upon his season-long observations of Costa. "He can lose it completely and for three seconds he's ready to kill, but then it's all over and he's the sweetest guy in the world."

The two became so close that Costa, somewhat miffed at the apparent lack of attention he was getting from Jorge Mendes, considered changing agents. Jesús García Pitarch, at Atlético, intervened. "I said: 'You need to show some gratitude to the people who have believed in you from the start. If anyone else but Jorge had called to tell me to go to Penafiel one Sunday morning to see some kid play, I wouldn't have considered it. He was a huge part of the Braga negotiations and he could have delayed things and waited for another club to show an interest. He could have insisted on a higher price. But he didn't and you should be grateful to him. Never forget where you've come from and the people who have helped you along the way. You can do what you want, but I don't think it would be fair to sack Jorge. And Antonio is a mate of mine! If that's who you're considering changing to then I'm happy for him, but I still think you owe Jorge something. He's the one who brought you from Brazil, who has helped you, made sure you have somewhere to live, a car – he may not call you very often but I can tell you he's been on the phone constantly to me, demanding to know why Celta owed you a month's money, telling me you needed more cash for a deposit for a house. You may not believe it, but that man is working hard for you.'"

It was enough to convince Costa to stick with Mendes. Alfaro, for his part, was not the type of person to steal another agent's player and did not pressurise the young Brazilian.

Eight games remained for the veteran Máximo Hernández, now caretaker coach, to steer the team to safety. Hernández knew from long experience that the key to the team's success would be keeping Costa motivated. "If you put everything you've got into this for the rest of the season and we avoid relegation, then you can take your holidays early at the end of the season," he promised the player. News of the unofficial deal was not well received elsewhere in the club and the president in particular thought his new coach had lost his mind. However, Hernández's incentive worked, as Rayo Vallecano were soon to discover to their cost.

"It was almost painful to watch," recalls Jesús García Pitarch of a match that would prove hugely influential on Costa's reputation at Atlético. "That was the day I knew we had been right to take a risk with him. That Rayo-Albacete game. I sat there thinking, 'this guy can really play'. He was all over them." Rayo were only two points from a promotion place when they ran into Costa. So well did he play that Tano Mora, a television commentator, christened him 'Curro Romero' after a famous Spanish bullfighter, although others preferred the possibly more apt 'Tasmanian Devil'.

Ripping through Rayo at will, he was directly responsible for two of the three goals Albacete scored that day and was on the point of scoring a fourth after brilliantly winning a penalty, but David Cobeño saved from 12 yards.

"García Pitarch came to see that match," remembers Hernández. "Before the game he asked me if Diego was going to play and I said: 'What the hell are you talking about? This team is Costa plus 10 more.'" You should have seen the look on Suso's face after the match. It said it all. I was screaming at him in delight. He knew he had a star on his hands."

Hernández was true to his promise and, as the end of the season approached with no threat of relegation, he told the Brazilian to start packing his bags. He did insist that, for the sake of appearances, Costa say that he was injured."

Hernández recognised that the player was more than ready to make the move up: "We talked a lot and he told me that he felt he was good enough for Atléti. He said that every time he was loaned out, it was like a knife in his heart. His dream was to go to Atléti and make his mark and he said that the moment they told him to pull on that jersey, he would start to make a difference there. He knew he had the talent and it spurred me on as well. He was determined to make it to the top and was doing everything he could to get there. He has such a strong character. There was a lot of humility too, but he was also very, very sure of himself.

"I thought he still had qualities he hadn't yet fully developed or applied to his game. And they only emerged through hard work and sheer balls. I kept on at him: 'You need to put your back into this, otherwise you'll never make it out of the second division,' and it pricked his pride. I told him that I'd give him a five at best for his performances, which had been average up till then. It was a risk and could have been too much for the boy but it was my way of motivating him. I saw that he needed a father figure as well as a coach. This was someone who still had a lot of growing up to do when he entered professional football. And the good thing about Diego is that he never once gave up, no matter how bad things got."

Costa had made his mark on Albacete in more ways than one. His team-mates and coaches not only speak of the impact he had on the team that season, but also, unanimously, remember him with genuine fondness.

Doctor Rodríguez Vellando remembers: "One of the kitmen, Antonio del Rey, had helped Diego out on a few occasions, including one day when he helped him break into his own house, the player having left his keys and his dog inside. The day he was leaving, Diego sought Antonio out, gave him a quick hug and slipped some money into his pocket. It was €1000. 'That's a thank you for all your help,' he said as he left."

Alberto Aguilar remembers, after moving to Córdoba, training at the Cerro del Espino, home to Atlético's reserve team. As he got off the bus, there was his old Albacete team-mate – already a star with the Atléti first team – waiting to catch up on old times.

Hernández was asked by Pitarch to report on Costa's contribution at the end of the season. "Pitarch asked me: 'Had he done more bad than good in his time with us?' I was absolutely clear – the lad had done far more good than bad. When we said goodbye I told him that I was convinced that he would be successful wherever he went. It was inevitable. And even now, for me, his potential is limitless."

"It was utterly amazing to see him play," says Alfaro. "Luis Aragonés used to say that some players look better than they are but in Diego's case, he's better than he looks. You could have cut his leg off on the football pitch and he'd stop, shove it back on and keep going. I have never been more impressed by any footballer. In 30 years they'll all still be talking about him in Albacete."

"Along with José Zalazar and Julián Rubio, he's probably the best player Albacete has ever had," adds Ferre de la Rosa.

5

VALLADOLID: COMING IN FROM THE COLD

'The impact of your army is like a grindstone against an egg. This is achieved by understanding strengths and weaknesses'

Sun Tzu, *The Art of War*

"IN 2009 PEOPLE started to sit up and notice Diego Costa, and we had to think hard about what his next move should be," says Jesús García Pitarch. "Even Barcelona wanted to buy him and their technical secretary, Albert Valentín, called to say, 'What are your plans for him? I really like him – he looks like he's got a bit of talent. We'd like him for Barca B'.

"'Yes, I like him too. That's why we bought him,' I told him. 'And I'm not going to sell him to you, firstly because I think this lad can go far and secondly because it makes no sense for me to sell him to you for €3m now. Better for me to wait five years and then you can have him for €40m.'"

Valentín and Barcelona did not know, however, that Atlético were having problems with Costa in the summer of 2009.

García Pitarch: "He turned up 10 days late for pre-season training, and then only after I had shouted and screamed down the phone at him. And when he did come back he was six or seven kilos overweight. The first thing he said to me was, 'Why should I bother? You obviously don't really rate me and I'd be happier if you'd just let me go'.

"'Ok let me show you how highly we rate you,' I told him. 'How many years do you want? Four? Five? You tell me. We'll draw up the contract here and now.'

"'Well … I don't know about that. I'd need to talk to my agent first,' he mumbled.

"I was furious. 'I see, first you tell me that Atléti doesn't rate you and then, when I say you can dictate the terms of your own contract, all of a sudden you need to talk it over with your agent. We couldn't do much more to show you how much we value you!'

"He had also handed me the contact number of a guy from a club in Brazil, Vitória in the Bahia state I think it was. He had talked to the club and he wanted us to either let him go free or loan him to them. Apparently this guy would be phoning me soon to discuss terms. He had come back absolutely determined to leave Atléti because we 'didn't value him'.

"We talked him round in the end. I sent the contract to Jorge Mendes and he approved it, although he didn't then come to witness the player sign it. Costa did that alone, with myself and Clemente Villaverde in attendance. I remember him saying, 'I'm only signing because of Suso. He believes in me'. It's unfortunate but it's just the way he is. He sees red for 10 seconds and then he calms down and turns back into the lovable guy he is, ready to listen to sense and make amends.

"Once we were on good terms again he confessed that he didn't want to spend the entire pre-season with Atléti, only to be loaned out at the last minute. That's what had happened the two previous years and he explained that it was hard to settle down at the new club when he arrived at the last minute. Usually there was also someone else in his position when he got there. 'I'd prefer just to go now, if I'm going,' he said. We understood completely and made sure that things happened quickly after that. He was off to Valladolid."

The move came from the Valladolid president, Carlos Suárez. Costa's progress was now a priority for Atlético, and the parent club sought assurances from Valladolid that their player would not spend the season on the bench. Suárez told García Pitarch that Costa was an important part of their plans and – unlike his previous loans – this time his contract would be picked up by the club for which he was playing. More than that, on paper at least, this would be a permanent transfer. A deal to take Sergio Asenjo from Valladolid to Atlético had already been struck, and Costa's move in the opposite direction was included in that agreement.

García Pitarch clarifies the technicalities: "Of course, the verbal agreement was that we'd be buying him back. In essence it was all smoke and mirrors, a way to ensure that the player felt committed to his new club. We did a lot of 'concealed loans' in those days."

Costa did not enjoy the upheaval that accompanied each move. "This is the last time I do this," he told his friends.

García Pitarch was also aware of the potentially negative impact on the player. "There was definitely a risk that all this moving about could actually have a detrimental effect on his performance. So we made sure we talked to him regularly. I went to see him play when I could and other technical staff went over a lot. I always told them to pop in and see him at the hotel, let the lad know that we were behind him. Of course it wasn't just Diego in that position. We visited all the players we had out on loan – Mario Suárez in Mallorca, for example."

For the first time since coming to Spain, Costa was able to spend most of the summer adapting to his new club, and even played in Valladolid's first competition of the season, the Teresa Rivero. This would have been impossible in previous seasons, when he would still have been stuck at Atlético's training ground, waiting for his next move. Almost immediately he began to show why, after two seasons in the Segunda, he belonged at the elite level. "He was so hungry," smiles Roberto Lago. "I had been one of his best mates at Celta, but he showed me absolutely no mercy when we met in a pre-season friendly."

The Uruguayan Fabián Canobbio had played with Costa at Celta Vigo and was now reunited with him at Valladolid. "When I first met him he was just a kid, although he clearly had a lot of talent. But when I saw him at Valladolid, I could see that he had really matured. Obviously he still possessed that amazing skill with the ball, but he had really grown up as a person." However, Costa didn't figure in Valladolid's first league game in Almería, with coach José Luis Mendilibar opting for another recent recruit, Manucho, signed from Manchester United, instead.

The club's star summer signings, Manucho and Alberto Bueno, had cost a combined €6m. Costa had his work cut out initially and struggled a bit in pre-season. The step up from the Segunda was not insignificant but he slowly started to establish himself.

"I remember him saying that since he was just here on loan, he didn't expect to get much playing time," confesses Borja Fernández, one of Costa's new team-mates that summer. "He thought that Manucho would be first-choice striker. And I told him that, with his talent, he would definitely get to play."

Luckily for Costa, the coach agreed. "Manucho was our big-name signing because he had come from United, but in no time at all I was choosing Costa over him."

Against the odds the two rivals, who shared their native language of Portuguese (Manucho is from Angola), formed a close friendship. "I called him *veado* [Portuguese slang, derogatory to homosexuals]," grins

Manucho. "He'd come after me but couldn't do much damage because I'm much bigger than he is. We used to play our music non-stop in the dressing room and loved dancing to *axé*, which is a kind of Brazilian pop music. We used to eat together a lot and loved *feijoada* [Brazilian bean stew with pork and beef]. We just had a brilliant time. He was a real joker, always hiding people's boots and flip-flops."

The two friends were often joined by a compatriot of Costa, the defender Nivaldo. "I ate with them at their favourite Brazilian restaurant a couple of times and listened to them talk a mix of Spanish and Portuguese whilst they wolfed down their *picanha*, a kind of barbecued meat." Nivaldo, who was an expert in the capoeira, a Brazilian martial art which combines dance and acrobatics, was often the butt of the others' jokes. Costa and Manucho took great delight in clambering all over each other trying to imitate the intricate moves of the capoeira, with hilarious results.

Costa was in the starting line-up for Valladolid's second league game of the season, at home against Valencia, and was a regular starter from then on, scoring six goals in his first 12 games.

"By our fifth or sixth game that season [José Luis] Mendilibar was saying that we had the best striker in Spain in terms of finding and using space," remembers Borja. "He said that there was nobody else to compare. If you were under pressure in the middle of pitch, you always looked for Diego and put the ball in his direction."

The prevailing opinion at the time was that Costa could not function as a pure No.9, but instead needed another striker beside him to take advantage of the work he was doing. However, Mendilibar's tactic was to pick out Costa with a pass whether he'd dropped wide to the wing or was making a solo run down the middle.

The local press was unanimous about the Brazilian's performance against Athletic Bilbao on October 5: "Diego Costa had a spectacular game and was a real headache for the men from Bilbao."

The striker spoke with reporters afterwards. "I put everything I've got into the game and was completely knackered afterwards because the coach likes us to press high so that we can get the ball and go for a counter-attack. I don't stick to one area and like to move a lot, looking for space on the wings and creating space for my team-mates."

Costa now realised that his place in the team on Sunday was dependent on his work rate and level of concentration midweek in training.

"Initially Diego got on best with Alberto Marcos and me," recalls Borja. "Marcos was like a father-figure in the team. I'm sure we would have been relegated in previous years if it hadn't been for him. He could see that Diego was special so he made a point of having a little chat with him right at the start of the season. After that, he didn't have to intervene. Diego completely understood. "

"I gave him a hard time," admits Marcos, now the club's director of football. "'I hear that you like to mess about,' I said to him. He looked at me and said, 'No I'm not like that, I swear. I'll show you Marcos'. Basically we had brought this 20-year-old Brazilian into the *Primera* and I couldn't see it working out. Fortunately however, I was completely wrong and it turned out that Diego was a real grafter who, despite being here on loan, was totally committed to the team. We were grateful because you always worry about guys who come into the team like that. He could have taken a back seat with the media for example, but he was always ready to speak up for the team. He joined us for pre-season training and we were all saying, 'Shit, this guy can run!'

"We nicknamed him *Locomotora* (the engine). And he won his place in the team in no time at all. He had come with a bit of a reputation, sure, but we saw none of that. He lived close to the stadium, opposite the players' living quarters and it took all of a minute and a half for him to get to the ground. He took this move very seriously and respected the fact that he was now in the *Primera*."

There was a special chemistry between Costa and Mendilibar from the start and the player has since called him the toughest coach he has ever worked under. Mendilibar even once sent Costa to a vineyard to pick grapes as punishment for a breach of discipline.

"He's like a father to me. He's got a foul temper and demands the earth from his players, but he also gives us freedom," he told the press at the time. This 'tough love' suited the player down to the ground and Costa even admitted that, if left to his own devices, his work rate at training would dramatically decline.

"Under Mendilibar, training sessions were very, very intense and Costa outdid us all," remembers the goalkeeper Fabricio Agosto.

True to form however, the striker had already had one or two run-ins with referees before the Christmas break and earned his fifth yellow of the season on December 20, during a game against Sporting. Refusing to be substituted, Costa had sprinted off to the other end of the pitch, making no attempt to disguise his intentions. "We've never see you move so fast," one journalist told him after the game.

Mendilibar regularly complained publicly about the excessively harsh treatment of Costa by referees every weekend. "He hasn't changed very much from that period," explains Mendilibar. "That bad temper was what drove him. He went onto the pitch ready to kill and then the referees would admonish him for every last thing he did. That's what happens when you're part of a little team like ours. I'd sit there on the bench grinding my teeth and slamming my foot on an imaginary brake.

"You can see he's still an impetuous guy, but he was even more so then. He was just so young when he came to us. And the qualities he has that wind-up his opponents these days would probably have frustrated Costa himself back then. My only doubt was whether he could overcome all the obstacles and make the most of his innate talent. The first time I saw him he looked a bit clumsy and pretty poor technically, but I quickly realised my mistake. This is a hugely talented player."

Following a disappointing draw at home against Almería, during which Costa had been denied a clear penalty, the club decided to sack Mendilibar.

"I said to Diego, 'Without you in the team, they'd have kicked me out in November or December,'" says the coach.

El País had heaped praise on the player just days before, on the eve of the visit of Barcelona: "In times of crisis teams look for a beacon of hope and this season Diego Costa has been a ray of light for Valladolid."

His performances had not been enough to save the coach, however. "Whenever we get together and talk about that season, Diego always says that Mendi is one of the coaches who has had the greatest impact on him," says Borja. "And he really believes that if the club hadn't sacked him like that we would have saved the season."

Mendilibar was replaced by Onésimo Sánchez who, until then, had been in charge of the club's youth team.

"In Diego I saw a player with huge potential. He was supremely talented but still had a long way to go to reach his best," remembers Onésimo. "He had this amazing physique and really stood out from the other players. We had a special bond immediately because I had also been a striker and during that period he made huge strides in his technical and tactical skills. I organised special training sessions specifically for him and he always insisted I stay and watch. He was desperate to improve.

Inevitably the new coach also saw the other side of Costa's character. Onésimo explains: "He's the type of player who actually needs that rage to play well and a more laid back Diego would only be 20% of what he is. In fact, as a coach, you need to calm him down rather than risk firing him up any further. I saw that side of him as more of a virtue than a flaw although, I have to say, I was ready to kill him the day he left us with 10 men against Espanyol."

That day referee Pérez Lasa sent the Brazilian off during a scoreless draw after he, according to the official's report, "stamped violently on an opposition player [Dídac Vilà] whilst play was halted". This was Costa's first red of a season he would end with a total of 11 cards.

The following week even the press noticed a downturn in Costa's mood following the incident: "Yesterday Diego Costa was visibly affected as he left training. Declining to slide down the banisters as he usually does, [press officer Mario Miguel used to say to him 'Diego, careful! Your legs pay my wages!'] he ignored all attempts at friendly banter and left without making any statement. Instead, captain Pedro López addressed the media. 'He's really pissed off because he left us with 10 men and that really hurt. It feels awful for any player to let his team down.'"

Jesús García Pitarch, the director of football back at Atlético, was encouraged to see his prodigy reacting differently after his transgressions. "He was maturing, becoming more responsible."

Costa only scored once under Onésimo but it was during perhaps his best performance at Valladolid. It was the kind of match that would become his signature – carrying the game to the opposition defence single-handedly, charging down the pitch and testing the goalkeeper at every opportunity with venomous shots.

There was forbearance, too. Zaragoza coach, José Aurelio Gay, had instructed his defenders, Marko Babić and Matteo Contini, to adopt roughhouse tactics with the Brazilian. Costa ended the game with a collarbone injury after a particularly nasty tackle from Contini.

Borja: "I actually told Gay after the game that I'd been surprised to see a team of his play such a dirty game and he replied that he had had no choice. The Zaragoza defence was incapable of stopping Costa any other way. I also remember that nobody heard a word of complaint from Diego. He saw the hard tackles as an occupational hazard."

"I hope that people now realise that Diego takes a lot of stick on the pitch, that he wins a lot of fouls and that because of how tough he is there are many more fouls on him not given when they should be," the coach told the press after the match. In fact, he was the most-fouled player in the team and the La Liga player who had drawn the second-highest number of bookings for fouls against him, after Jesús Navas.

Despite the Brazilian's efforts though, things were going badly for the team. With only one win in 10 games (at the Riazor on March 20), the club decided it was time for another change of coach. This time they opted for a more pragmatic appointment and chose Javier Clemente. The no-nonsense coach told the press that he was "sick of sitting at home with no job", adding, "Don't worry, I *can* make a silk purse out of a sow's ear". He said he had come to light a fire under the team and drag them out of the mire of relegation.

"I could fill a book with all the Clemente stories from those two months," smiles Borja. "At first we thought he was a bit detached, wrapped up in his own world, but we quickly realised that he knew everything that happened at the club."

"I remember one day Baraja, Diego and I were discussing tactics with him. Every time we mentioned Diego he would ask who we were talking about. It turned out he only knew him as 'Costa' or 'Costinha'. Diego thought it was hilarious – the two of them really hit it off because Clemente knew how to handle him," adds Fabricio.

Kitman Óscar Fernández remembers more of the coach's gaffes. "He spent a month calling Nauzet Alemán 'Pedro López' and mixed Manucho's name up with 'Maniche'. Eventually someone told him and Clemente bit his head off, saying that he would bloody well call people whatever name he felt like."

The team started to improve under the former Spain manager. The odds were against them in terms of survival in the *Primera* and Clemente made a strategic decision to get the two players he saw as his most dangerous on the pitch, together, whenever possible. Having spent most of the season sharing the single striker role, now Manucho and Costa joined forces. Costa, not for the first time in his career, was designated a secondary role in the forward line, frequently moving to the right.

The more aggressive gameplan worked and Valladolid began to believe in their own escape. However, their final game of the season was a trip to the Camp Nou to face Barcelona, who needed to win to ensure victory over Real Madrid in the championship race. Clemente joked in the build-up to the game that he would call on favours from Pep Guardiola, the coach of Barcelona who he managed in the national team, or Ángel María

Villar, his old boss at the Spanish FA, to have the match cancelled.

There was no reprieve, however. Valladolid fared no worse than many opponents of Guardiola's team in their 4-0 defeat, but it left them in the third and final relegation position in La Liga, a single point behind Málaga.

Nobody was more upset in the aftermath than Costa. He put his arms around Baraja, and it was impossible to tell which was the four-year veteran with Real Valladolid now considering a season in the *Segunda* and which was the itinerant gun-for-hire, loaned out for a seemingly never-ending series of relegation battles.

It had been a tough year in another new home for Costa. Despite his many friendships at Valladolid, the northern climate had proven to be his enemy. He would train in a balaclava, and long trousers, with multiple pairs of gloves. "His hands were frozen solid and he could hardly walk at times because of the chilblains in his feet," recalls his team-mate Alberto Marcos.

Costa would apply strong heat cream on his feet and lower legs as he fought conditions far removed from Lagarto. The cream eventually burned the skin on his feet and calves.

"On another occasion his feet were so frozen that he couldn't play. We had to put him in the Jacuzzi, then the sauna," remembers Óscar Fernández. "He couldn't even get his boots on, poor guy. His feet were purple. He had to wear flip flops for a week. I took the piss out of him waddling about like a duck and he blew his top, 'It's not funny you bastard!'"

During the season Costa had moved into an apartment immediately adjacent to the stadium. His team-mates would wake early and drive through the cold to get to training. As they pulled up, they would see Costa behind his window and in the warm hug of his central heating, still in his pyjamas, grinning and waving.

When he left Valladolid, the story was the same as it had been at Celta Vigo and Albacete. The reputation which preceded him had made way for total respect as a team-mate and, ever more so, as a player.

"You could see he was totally committed," recalls Marcos, who was a good friend by the end. "He's the kind of footballer I really enjoy playing with. He leads from the front, never backs down and always has your back. All the temper you see on the pitch disappears the minute he's back in the dressing room. At times he struggles to express himself but when he does share, he's very entertaining. He can be a bit shy at the start, but once he trusts you, he's very open and direct. Diego's old school – what happens on the pitch, stays on the pitch. He can have a bust-up with you and be close to killing you and then, a few hours later you're having dinner together. It's like he steps into another world when he plays but he never leaves the field looking to get even. He just doesn't hold grudges.

"He was very young when he came to Valladolid, but surprisingly mature. We had a tough situation in the dressing room and probably asked him for a lot more than was reasonable."

"He carried us," adds Fabricio. "We depended on him and I think he knew it. I used to say to myself at training sessions, 'What the hell is this guy doing here?'"

Valladolid director Jesús Dominguez: "He wasn't quite as good then as he is today but you could see he had the potential. In fact, Eloy de la Pisa, sports editor of *El Norte de Castilla* newspaper, believed that he was as good as Messi. There's a saying that 'victory has a hundred fathers and defeat is an orphan' but that season things were different. Although there were very few people who could take on responsibility for Valladolid's relegation, Diego Costa was completely blameless."

And once more, he left his team-mates and coaching staff lighter of pocket than when he had arrived – Costa had lost none of his talent for poker. "We used to play to while away the time on long journeys and he usually beat me. Come to think of it, he usually beat everyone," chuckles Clemente. "He wiped us all out," confirms Fabricio.

Costa was developing. Mendilibar remembers a player who was without peer in the league in terms of his physical capabilities ("My advice is to avoid any kind of face-off with him. He almost never comes off worse from those situations") but who lacked composure in front of goal. Onésimo, the second of the three coaches that season and the one under whom Costa hardly featured, also recalled how hurt the young striker would be when criticised.

And all the while, Atlético were watching and waiting. During the 2009-10 season, they bought the remainder of Costa's rights from Braga. In January 2010, the Atlético player Mariano Pernía was filmed discussing the Brazilian striker the day before a Valladolid-Atlético match. "There is no doubt that when he comes back he'll be captain in no time. He's super smart – if he wasn't he couldn't play like that. There were times that he had to miss training because of some injury or other. And then he'd play a game and he'd be the best player on the pitch."

Pernía's words were to be borne out within months. Diego Costa's apprenticeship was complete. It was time for him to prove himself at Atlético Madrid.

6

ATLÉTICO: THE BREAKTHROUGH

'If you know yourself and the enemy well enough,
then you should not fear the outcome of a hundred battles'

Sun Tzu, *The Art of War*

IN THE SUMMER of 2010 Atlético Madrid were under serious financial pressure. One of the counter measures raised by the chief executive, Miguel Ángel Gil, was the sale of Diego Costa, just back from yet another season-long loan with his reputation further enhanced. With Sergio Agüero and Diego Forlán leading a long roster of forwards, a deal at the right price would not be opposed by Gil.

Antonio Alfaro, the agent who had engineered a previous loan for Costa, now offered the striker to José Manuel Llaneza at Villarreal, but there was no interest. Quique Pina at Granada suggested a €6m transfer through the club's owners at Udinese in Italy, but the price was too low. Zaragoza, Málaga, Getafe, Betis and Sevilla were all interested in a loan, but neither club nor player wanted another season-long deal.

Jesús García Pitarch, then in his final season as director of football, recalls: "I knew that whoever got him would be hitting the jackpot and if anyone had been willing to pay €8m for him Atlético would definitely have sold him. But no-one was prepared to pay that much."

Once again Costa was to test the patience of the people who had backed him so far and June arrived with no sign of the Brazilian at pre-season training. Eventually he appeared, four days late and out of shape.

"Blame my mum, she's far too good a cook," was his initial explanation.

"He tried to avoid the cameras us much as possible and insisted that we didn't film his whole body," recalls journalist José David Palacio.

Visibly upset, the player struggled through a public apology, explaining that his late arrival had been caused by a simple misunderstanding.

"It was just a breakdown in communication. I lost my Spanish mobile and didn't realise that the club don't have my Brazilian number. Otherwise they could have called me on that. But I came back the minute they got in touch and I'm really sorry this has happened. Something seems to go wrong every year. Problems seem to seek me out. I was actually waiting to hear from my agent to tell me to come to Spain because I was desperate to get back to work. I was getting really bored on holiday. Next time I'll make sure my ticket is booked three or four days in advance."

The player threw himself into pre-season training and more or less fasted for seven days. Having watched

Costa drop several kilos, Atlético head coach Quique Sánchez Flores began to have renewed confidence in his striker.

Defender Álvaro Domínguez remembers the Brazilian's shaky start. "Initially the coaching staff was not impressed. He was badly out of shape when he arrived and completely off form. When Diego takes a holiday he really goes for it but once he starts training again, he also gives it 100%. After just two weeks he was like a machine again."

Midfielder Juan Valera worked with Costa over three pre-seasons. "He was one of the players who was always about to be transferred elsewhere, someone who was about to leave the club. But you could see how fit he was, a force to be reckoned with. When he was in good shape he trained like a beast. The thing that he tended to neglect was 'invisible training' – following a healthy diet, getting lots of rest and developing an understanding of his own body. He was a bit scatter-brained, but that's just his way. He's a one-off. He would get distracted and, if we'd been told to do an exercise twice, he'd end up doing it three times."

Soon, the other members of the Atléti squad in the early days of pre-season were stunned at how quickly the overweight Brazilian shed the excess kilos and once again began to pound his team-mates in training. He had a lot to prove to himself, his team-mates and the coaching staff, but by the next time he spoke to reporters, he appeared certain that he would not start the new season in the *Rojiblanco* shirt.

"It's up to me to prove that I'm good enough to stay but in reality I won't be surprised if they loan me out again," the player said.

This year, however, things would be different. Quique Sánchez Flores initially saw a straight choice between Costa and the Argentine winger Eduardo 'Toto' Salvio, both non-EU players competing for one of the three positions available. The coach favoured Salvio, but after the acquisition that summer of the Uruguayan centre-back Diego Godín, Sánchez Flores revisited his resources.

On August 19, Atlético confirmed that Salvio would be loaned to Benfica for the coming season, with the Portuguese club also acquiring a share of the player's rights. It was a hugely influential deal as far as Costa was concerned. Not only did it open up a place for one more non-EU player, but it also brought in money to ease the pressure for other transfers.

However, García Pitarch recalls there was still much debate about the wisdom of retaining a non-EU player to play back-up to the two stars of Atléti's front line. "We knew Diego had a battle on his hands because we already had two outstanding strikers in the team but the lad had earned his place and I reckoned he would get a good bit of playing time."

Quique Sánchez Flores' decision to stand by Costa had its roots in Atlético's match in Valladolid the previous season. "The whole squad was talking about him when he came back – they already knew he was lightning fast," says the coach.

"He tried to take it calmly," recalls Fran Mérida. "He knew that Agüero and Forlán were on another level. He just took it as an opportunity to learn."

The player himself said: "Those two are super-talented and work like dogs every day, so if I want to compete with them, I'll just have to do the same."

On August 27 Costa was an unused substitute for the UEFA Supercup final against Internazionale. Atlético – the previous season's Europa League champions – defeated the Champions League winners from Italy through goals from José Antonio Reyes and Agüero. The Brazilian may have missed out on any game time, but celebrated with his team-mates, finally a part of a winning team, albeit stuck behind its seemingly immoveable stars.

Costa made his debut for Atlético in a league match on August 30, coming on for Forlán for the last 23 minutes of a 4-0 rout of Sporting Gijón. Soon it was impossible to ignore him.

He scored five goals in his first 12 games and was already a regular starter by matchday four in La Liga. In Atlético's fifth game, against Zaragoza at home, he smashed home an assist from Filipe Luis for the winner. He scored against Rosenborg in the Europa League. Not long after however, Costa ran into trouble in the build-up to a Copa del Rey clash against Universidad de Las Palmas. Costa was rooming with Mérida, and both were down to start. A teamtalk was scheduled for 7.30am but both players overslept and arrived five minutes late. With this coach, not a good idea. "I don't tolerate this," he growled. "Sort yourselves out or I'll send you both home."

The trips away were an ideal opportunity for Costa to begin to put the squeeze on his team-mates through his poker skills. His room would almost always host Atléti's touring Texas Hold 'em game.

Paulo Assunção, Costa's fellow Brazilian, benefited from some Costa tips along the way. "One day the pair of us were playing with Silvio and a mate, who was cheating. Diego and I could see what he was up to so we didn't bet, but Silvio did. Then when we all turned our cards over, Diego burst out laughing and Silvio realised what had happened. He went mad at us – 'You bastards, I'm going to kill you!' We'd play for hours with Reyes and De Gea, although De Gea and Kun [Agüero] liked PlayStation, too."

There were punishments for the loser, like downing a litre of water in one and then jumping into the hotel swimming pool. "Diego did that one day – he's always up for it, whether he's playing football or Texas Hold'em," smiles Juanito.

As the season progressed, Costa's performances continued to surprise and impress. Despite this, he was often the target of discontented whistling from the Calderón crowd. Javier Hernández, the scout who first spotted Costa in Chaves, remembers the supporters' initial disapproval of a player who would rise in their affections above almost any other.

"It says a lot about how strong he is that he still managed to take a great leap forward in sporting terms. Some of my mates used to slag him off and tell me we had landed a no-hoper. They're not laughing now."

"I remember shortly after he arrived I went home and had to listen to my dad and my brothers criticising him for being clumsy," says Álvaro Domínguez. "I just told them that as soon he became more focused, he'd be a superb player. I knew that because he was impossible to play against in training. A total nightmare."

"People thought he was awkward and ungainly but he wasn't at all. We would play football-tennis in the dressing room and he always won," says team-mate Antonio López. "You could see that he had matured compared to previous years, when he'd start belting out some song in the middle of a team lunch."

The highlight of Costa's season was to be an unforgettable match against Osasuna in Pamplona on April 3. Agüero was suspended and Forlán, whose turbulent relationship with Quique Sánchez Flores was at an all-time low, had been left on the bench. The coach decided to give Costa his chance, and the Brazilian rewarded him with a performance that would stand as a landmark. It began with a spectacular clash with the goalkeeper Ricardo; Costa then waged war with the Osasuna defenders Lolo and Sergio Fernández, the latter ending up with a red card. The home side opened the scoring but the Brazilian was an unstoppable force and won the game with a first La Liga hat-trick.

"That was the best match I ever played with him," smiles Assunçáo. "Osasuna were defending high up the pitch and that's when he's at his most dangerous. Unbeatable really. He is so strong, so fast. Just like Ronaldo, his great idol."

García Pitarch agrees. "He won that match for them. It's what he does now every weekend but that was the day everyone realised that, with a bit of time and work, he was going to be an outstanding player."

Quique Sánchez Flores announced that day: "He has surpassed all our expectations of him."

Costa himself said: "Everything went perfectly for me out there."

The image of Costa scoring and then running to embrace Forlán, who was warming up on the touchline, was beamed throughout the country and the Spanish press celebrated with him. The next day's headline: 'Costa Vindicated'.

Costa was now the squad's most productive striker, with six goals in 1008 league minutes, averaging one every 168 minutes. In total, only two less than Forlán, who was still in the eye of a hurricane-like relationship with his coach, just months after scoring the goals that won the Europa League final.

Costa, however, had no interest in point-scoring. "Forlán congratulated me. He's a great guy who has always encouraged me and he's delighted for me."

The Uruguayan was equally generous. "Diego's a great team-mate. He may be too impulsive at times, but he's got a big heart."

Forlán's problems with Quique Sánchez Flores had merely opened a door for Costa. Given the opportunity, the striker proceeded to rip it from its hinges. As more was asked of him, the player who had been loaned out time and again, and who that very summer had been so close to leaving, found he had more to give.

"He hated leaving every summer, probably because he knew he was good enough to play for Atléti," says Antonio López. "He could have had a place in the first team much sooner than he did and I had to calm him down when he didn't get a game. The true merit of his season wasn't that Forlán was frozen out, but that Diego totally earned his place as the main striker."

"The minute he was trusted to play a key role in the team, his performances improved," says Juanito. "He just wanted to feel needed."

Costa – now regularly in short-sleeved shirts and gloves on matchdays – may have been finding a new gear, but Atlético's campaign had begun to lose momentum. They were sitting in the final European qualification slot in the league and had dropped out of the Europa League, left behind by Bayer Leverkusen and, surprisingly, beaten home and away by Aris Salonika in the group stage.

As if a stalling season wasn't bad enough, the first teamers had to get used to a new challenge in training. "Forlán and Agüero tried to avoid too much contact in training because they wanted to be totally match-fit, but Diego went into every practice session as if it were a league match," recalls Juanito.

Álvaro Domínguez: "I'd try to intimidate him and get in his face, and he'd look at me and say 'Okay, now it's your turn'. He'd never back down. He's a joy if he's on your team but if not, he's a total bastard. The more you push him the happier he is."

Juan Valera: "He used to whisper stuff under his breath to wind you up, although it was all meant as a joke. And if you retaliated by giving him a kick, he'd just laugh it off. He was always more hurt by harsh words than any kind of physical pain. He'd punch you and then when the referee whistled, give you a hug and apologise."

Paulo Assunção: "Sometimes Quique would warn him about his behaviour and say, 'Diego, you're heading for a booking'. But he knew his limits. He had matured a lot and had got to know the referees. He knew exactly what to say to them."

Costa, the clown prince of dressing rooms from

Valladolid in northern Spain to Braga in Portugal, finally took the crown at Atlético. He would trip passing team-mates, or pull their trousers down as they were in mid-conversation. He would play his music and show off his moves. He would dive-bomb the Jacuzzi. He would steal team-mates' socks.

Paulo Assunção: "One day we were all in the dressing room and Diego got a big bottle of water and put it on top of a newspaper showing a picture of a topless model. He called Maniche over and said, 'If you look through the bottle you'll see a naked woman'. Just as Maniche was bending over to take a look Diego squeezed the bottle and soaked him, saying, 'How on earth do you expect the poor girl to take her clothes off if you're watching?'"

Away from the pranks Costa was growing up. He had married Isa, his childhood sweetheart, who had remained for now in Brazil. Much of Costa's heart remained in his homeland and he still loved eating Brazilian dishes like *picanha*, and *feijoada*. His hometown of Lagarto was a frequent topic of conversation, as he reflected on how he loved going to the beach, eating burgers and going to concerts. "He always talked about the music from home and it was usually blaring out from his car," says Assunção. "In fact, I still have a mountain of records that he gave me. He was friendly with singers and bands at home and would always bring back their records from Brazil."

Assunção would eventually move to São Paulo in 2012, leaving Costa his Porsche Cayenne and a billiard table that was too big for his apartment. He remembers one other major event from this time, which again reveals a side to Costa which could scarcely be further removed from the on-field warrior. "Diego brought his Yorkshire terrier to Madrid but one day when he was parking and didn't realise the dog was behind the car, he reversed over it. He was devastated, totally depressed for a month. When I asked him why he was so low he practically broke down. 'I can't believe it. I killed my dog. He came out of the house to greet me and I didn't see him and I ran over him. How could I have killed my dog, Assu?' Since then he's bought two dogs but it took him a long time to get over that loss. Off the pitch he's so soft-hearted, I've never seen him have a cross word with anyone."

Diego Costa finished the 2010-11 season as the breakthrough act of a disappointing campaign for Atlético. The club finished seventh, squeaking into qualification for next season's Europa League, and Costa claimed eight goals in all competitions.

"I've had to fight and struggle all my life," he said at the end of the season. "It's part of me now and I'm going to keep on fighting."

He had no idea that his battle for a place at Atlético Madrid was far from over.

7

RAYO VALLECANO:
THE REPRIEVE

*'If, in the midst of difficulties we are always ready to seize
an advantage, we may extricate ourselves from misfortune'*

Sun Tzu, *The Art of War*

July 27, 2011. Costa has worked like a Trojan for three weeks. It is the last training session before Atlético's first game of the pre-season, a Europa League qualifier against the Norwegian side Strømsgodset. Costa has been deadly. The new coach, Gregorio Manzano, has been impressed.

During a routine crossing and finishing drill, Costa goes to strike the ball and his right leg twists badly, damaging the striker's knee.

After an initial examination in the Vicente Calderón's medical centre the initial prognosis is not good and Costa is immediately transferred to the FREMAP clinic for an MRI scan. The results could not be worse: a ruptured cruciate ligament plus meniscus damage. Immediate surgery. Six months out of football. Maybe seven.

Paulo Assunção: "I visited him in hospital and he was a bit low initially, but I kept encouraging him, telling him to get better quickly, and he would always perk up and tell me not to worry about him. 'It's meant to be,' he'd say. He refused to let things get to him and made an effort to accept what had happened. He was only in his early twenties, but you'd have said this was a guy in his thirties. He was so wise about it all. He accepted it and that made everything much easier for him."

What most of those around him, including the majority of his team-mates, didn't know was that Costa had been on the point of leaving Atlético Madrid when he was injured.

The player himself takes up the story. "Before training that afternoon my agent Jorge Mendes called to tell me I was going to Turkey. The club had accepted an offer from Besiktas and they were just waiting for my agreement. We spoke on the phone and then agreed to meet later at the hotel. Then I went to training and ended up with the injury. It was a serious one but I have always had faith in God and believe that each of us has his own destiny. So I kept calm about it. It must have happened for a reason. It was as if God was telling me he didn't want me to go to Turkey. I had to start again from scratch."

Instead of a new start in Turkey, Costa was embarking on a much tougher journey, and one he would have to undertake alone.

On the day of his operation Costa's team-mates, wearing vests with the words 'Ánimo, Diego' – Stay strong, Diego – scrawled across them, sealed a victory against Strømsgodset in the Vicente Calderón, two goals from Reyes giving them a flimsy 2-1 lead in the tie. Doctors Fernando García de Lucas, Gloria López and José Ramón Almoguera operated successfully on Costa's right knee.

Costa left the clinic three days later. He would now have to immobilise the leg and wear a splint for 10 days before the stitches could come out and physiotherapy could begin. Once the stitches were removed he began working in water to mobilise his joints and help his surgical scars heal. The final phase would involve cycling and running in the gym before he could think about playing football again.

The recuperation process went well. Óscar Pitillas, the club's fitness coach, worked intensively with Costa, who always seemed to hit his targets earlier than had been predicted by medical staff.

Sergio Asenjo, the goalkeeper, was also recovering from surgery at this time, but soon he was hurtling past his team-mate in terms of recovery and continuing his rehab work alongside the first team in the gym. He would push himself still further, leaping into the air, landing on that right leg. 'Don't do that!' they would shout, like concerned parents. 'Be careful!'

"He was just progressing so much faster than Asenjo because of his strong physique and the sheer power in his legs," laughs Assunção.

The next thing anyone knew, he was running up and down stairs. Then taking them two and three at a time.

Pitillas would run after him shouting, "Do you want them to sack me or what?"

As January 2012 approached, Costa was nearly ready to take to the training pitch and get back to work. The only question that remained was where that might be.

To his great relief the answer came in the form of a timely phone call from Rayo Vallecano coach José Ramón Sandoval.

"I've watched you training at Atlético and I want you in my team. I trust you and you should trust me. If you come here and give your very best, then you'll be a star player at Rayo."

Costa responded: "Nobody has ever spoken to me like that before. You're on."

Levante, who had hoped to unite Costa with his former manager Juan Ignacio Martínez, lost out on the deal and a slim, toned Costa joined fellow Atléti team-mates Joel Robles and Jorge Pulido en route to Vallecas. Back at the Calderón the rest of the squad were getting acquainted with Diego Simeone, who had replaced Manzano some weeks before.

Costa had not kicked a ball before his first session with his new team-mates, and began that day with one-on-one work with the fitness coach. By the halfway point in the session, he was waved into the main population, and immediately set about showing the Rayo players who they had signed.

"He had very few real difficulties and things went more

quickly and more smoothly than we expected," recalls the Rayo Vallecano football director Felipe Miñambres. "A club like ours has to take risks with players, but his injury didn't set us back at all. He was going to slot in really well with the other strikers, Raúl Tamudo and Michu. We wanted to give him a bit of time however and were not planning to use him for the first month."

On January 25, 2012, Costa was officially presented as a Rayo player, wearing his by now traditional No.19.

He told the press: "I'm still not 100%, but I'm down to the right weight."

"You're skinnier now than you were when you were playing," one journalist told the player.

"I suppose he came here to test himself," says Roberto Trashorras, the midfielder who had joined Rayo from Celta that season. "Diego obviously understood that this was his big opportunity to prove that he was worthy of Atléti."

"You certainly couldn't tell that he'd just recovered from a serious injury," recalls Míchel, the Rayo midfielder. "He came in like a charging bull. No way was he going to need a few weeks to get on board, like we thought. In fact, we were all more concerned about his knee than he was."

"We saw exactly what he was made of in that first training session," says midfielder Javi Fuego. "Sandoval told him to take it easy and he said to him, 'Let's see what happens. If my knee's okay then it will cope. If not, it will be too much and it'll break again'. Classic Diego!"

And Rayo needed Costa in the team as soon as possible. Sandoval knew it, and acted quickly.

Rayo were due to play a vital game against Zaragoza on February 5 in the Romareda and Sandoval had decided that the Brazilian should travel with them. Few expected him to get any game time at all, and nobody counted on him playing 45 minutes.

Within half an hour Zaragoza were ahead by a goal from Hélder Postiga and Rayo had lost Trashorras through injury. Sandoval's men were in real trouble. At half-time the coach asked Costa: "Can you cope with the second half?"

"No sweat. Thought you'd never ask," replied Costa.

The striker replaced Rayco. "I'd been told that I'd get 20 minutes that day, but I ended up playing half the match, basically because there was no-one else," remembers Costa.

He was taking a risk in going on so soon, but the gamble paid off. Within 30 minutes, Casado crossed from the left and Costa responded with a fierce finish past Roberto. Before that, however, he had already produced another of his trademarks – two yellow cards, one each for Costa and Paredes, for scrapping with each other. Fiery, free-scoring Costa was back.

"Winning is what matters but I'm delighted that I could have helped by getting a goal. There's no better confidence boost. I'm dedicating the goal to Óscar Pitillas who has been a tower of strength for the last six months and to everyone at Rayo who have shown so much faith in me," he told the press after the game.

The coach publicly acknowledged the risk he had taken in playing Costa. "The medics weren't keen on him playing too long in his debut match but they left it up to me. Diego changed the whole match. He made mincemeat of their defence and was very dangerous every time he touched the ball."

Back in the dressing room, coach Sandoval was less restrained. He grabbed Costa by the back of the neck and the two men bumped heads.

Costa was firing on all cylinders. Thinner and more toned, he threw himself into his work and scored four goals in his first three games, as Rayo picked up nine valuable points.

"I couldn't ask for more," he said. "I really didn't expect to be as fit as this after being injured for so long. But I'm getting better and better every day and I love being here at Rayo. I have never felt stronger."

Back in the Atlético dressing room, Costa was not forgotten. Fran Mérida explains: "If we were listening to the radio in the bus and heard that Diego had scored, we'd all start cheering and clapping. Simeone was blown away by the reaction!"

Costa had recently become a father and dedicated most of his goals to his baby daughter.

"You could see from the very first match that he was too good for us. He was unstoppable." says Míchel. Goalkeeper Dani Giménez agrees: "I would watch him and say to myself, 'What the hell is this guy doing at Rayo?' He was head and shoulders above us all and I was astounded that a player of that quality had been loaned out."

Costa had performed well in his first matches, but the best was yet to come. In his fourth game for the club, Madrid came to Vallecas and Costa took the fight to their superstar defenders.

"That battle with Pepe and Sergio Ramos was epic," recalls Giménez. "I'd never seen anything like it before. In a game against a big side like them you don't see a lot of the ball, your possession usually comes from rebounds and scraps, but he made a virtue out of all that."

In the end Real Madrid scraped a 1-0 victory thanks to a cool little backheel from Cristiano Ronaldo. The game had been like a bare-knuckle fight with many controversial moments.

"It's not often that you start believing Madrid are beatable but that day it really felt like we had a chance," recalls Alejandro Arribas, a young centre-back in that Rayo team. "It's when his thing with Sergio Ramos started. He just did the same things as usual, but it was against Madrid so it got noticed. We all knew that this was the repertoire he trotted out every game."

Rayo protested that referee David Fernández Borbalán, who sent Michu off for a bad tackle on Sami Khedira, had failed to see a Ramos elbow on Costa inside the box.

"It's the club badge that the referees look at," claimed Costa later. "Sure I fought with Madrid players from the get-go, but what happens on the pitch, stays on the pitch."

Costa's own team-mates accosted him throughout the game, trying to persuade him to turn down the intensity ever so slightly.

Soon the Rayo players realised that they, too, had to deal with the dervish who had taken it to Pepe and Ramos. Every day, in training.

Míchel: "On the pitch, if he can do you some damage then he will, but later the two of you might end up hanging out, going for a drink – and there will be absolutely no problem."

Labaka: "He actually likes people kicking him. He needs that. Okay, at times he lets things get out of hand but that's not out of badness, it's just his sheer determination to win."

Dani Pacheco: "Sometimes I'd make some jokey comment whilst we were changing and he'd find it hilarious then I'd say something similar out on the pitch and he'd give me a filthy look."

Alejandro Arribas had an interesting relationship with Costa during the Brazilian's half-season at Rayo.

As a starting centre-back, Arribas was often a direct opponent of Costa in training sessions, which was almost the same as being a direct opponent of the Brazilian during matchday. At the same time, the two were near neighbours in Las Matas and would share the journey in Costa's car – the striker driving, the defender providing directions. Arribas, more than any other player, quickly understood the Jekyll and Hyde nature of his team-mate.

"He doesn't know how else to play football," laughs Arribas. "The pair of us would be at each other's throats at training and then off we'd go together quite happily at the end. I couldn't believe the way he changed on and off the pitch. He'd be in a foul mood the minute he had the ball at his feet and then afterwards, as nice as nine pence. Of course, what really took my breath away was his talent. I had never played with such a good footballer. I've played against him a few times since then and we always exchange jerseys. People occasionally ask me how to stop him and I tell them that I've no idea."

On the pitch, Costa found his team in a familiar position, with the threat of relegation ever present. It was going to be a heart-stopping second half to the season and after a solid start post-Christmas they began to falter. A run of eight defeats in nine at the end of the season – the exception was a 6-0 win over Osasuna featuring a beautiful individual goal by Costa – left them on the precipice. Just as in the striker's season with Valladolid, it came down to the last game of the season.

Matchday 38 saw Rayo at home in the old Teresa Rivero stadium against Granada. Both teams were in a group of four in danger of filling the final relegation position at the close of play. Costa's Atlético team-mates were away at another team in the mix, Villarreal. Arribas remembers a level of anxiety before the game unlike any other he has experienced. It carried out onto the pitch. Neither team could put anything together. Costa, desperate to make a difference, could not force a breakthrough.

Radamel Falcao scored at Villarreal to put Atléti 1-0 ahead. A goal for Rayo now would send Villarreal down and save Rayo. The injured Dani Giménez moved behind the Granada goal to urge his team-mates on as the match entered three minutes of added time.

Referee Undiano Mallenco blew for a Rayo corner. Cobeño, the goalkeeper, ran up to join the attack and the ball was sent into the box but Granada's defenders cleared it. It was launched back in and Michu got a touch, but it bounced back off the post. The ball was in front of an open goal and it was all about who would react first. This time, it was not the emerging star of La Liga, Diego Costa, but 34-year-old former Spain international Raúl Tamudo, in his one and only season at Rayo, who had come off the bench to head the ball over the line. 1-0. Ecstasy. The veteran hero ran away with his shirt thrown up in the air.

The whole of Vallecas leapt up in one great roar of joy and embraced each other. Several of the players collapsed on the ground, unable to cope with the agonising pressure of the last few minutes and coach Sandoval fell to his knees, a glazed look in his eyes as the fans ran on the pitch to join the celebrations. Rayo were staying up.

Costa and Arribas, training-ground adversaries, car poolers and team-mates, embraced on the pitch.

Costa was due back at Atlético the next day, but was not going to miss the celebrations that followed this great escape.

Giménez: "It was an incredible couple of hours, unbelievable. Everyone went mad; people were being grabbed and thrown up in the air. We were so relieved and delighted, especially since people had begun to question the players' commitment. Diego had given us 100% and more. In fact, he ended up playing a few games with an injury. You'd see him hare about the pitch on Sunday and say, 'Wasn't he having trouble with his knee during the week?' It was amazing."

"I was captain and I'll always remember the strength and support he gave us at a very difficult time," says Míchel. "I was astonished that a player would come from Atléti and be prepared to leave his guts on the pitch for us."

Having started every game except his debut, Costa's

time at Rayo proved to be a critical turning point in his career, as the player explained.

"I had messed about a bit in the past but something just clicked for me and I was determined to come back better than ever. It wasn't anything physical that changed. It was more my mental attitude. And Sandoval really helped. He gave me a lot of confidence, just like Mendilibar at Valladolid. I got such a warm welcome at Vallecas and everyone was great to me. I can honestly say that it changed my life."

Trashorras: "His metamorphosis into an elite player started here. Our style of football really suited him and he shone whenever he played. He adapted immediately and was totally committed from the start. He never went on about what he was going to do in the future, never really mentioned Atléti. He was focused on playing for us and I think he saw this as a chance for people to see him for what he was."

This time there was a new element in the testimonials coming from his team-mates after a loan. As before, there emerged the image of a no-limits competitor and a prankster, of a talent on the brink of blossoming. Now, though, there was also a new respect around the conditions in which the loan to Rayo came about. Here was a player whose right knee had been in pieces at the start of the season, yet who had pushed his body to the limit to help his temporary team-mates achieve their goal. He had been given a strict limit on his body weight in order to avoid placing the knee under excess pressure, and he stuck to this completely. He played through injuries that were a legacy of his operation and rehab. He never took the edge of his game. This is how his team-mates remember him.

"He transformed himself physically and put on a lot of muscle," says Cobeño. "And it made a huge difference to his football. You know, I think Diego became much more self-confident at Rayo. And thanks to him, we managed to stay up. Both parties came out of it well, let's put it like that."

"My only regret is that he was at Rayo for just six months," says Míchel, the captain and himself a club legend. "Along with Guilherme [another Brazilian striker], [Elvir] Bolić and Bolo he is the best player Rayo has ever had."

"Right up to the very last moment of the transfer market we tried to get him back at Rayo for the next season," reveals Felipe Minámbres, Rayo's director of football. "And until the moment that Atléti won the UEFA Supercup we had a chance. But that game was on the same day as the market closed so that was that. We like to think that we made our own small contribution to his evolution, the transformation he went through. He and I still talk from time to time. He loves talking about football. It's nice that he's been one of us and it's great to have been a small part of his amazing journey."

8

ATLÉTICO: KINGS OF
THE BERNABÉU

*'The commander is the chief arbiter of the people's fate,
the man who dictates whether the nation shall live
in peace or peril'*

Sun Tzu, *The Art of War*

DESPITE THE FACT that Diego Costa's stock had
soared whilst at Rayo Vallecano, the Brazilian returned
to pre-season training at Atlético ahead of the 2012-
13 campaign with much left to prove. There were still
those yet to be convinced of the player's talent, not
least coach Diego Pablo'*El Cholo*' Simeone, who had
completely altered the mentality and the expectations
of his team since taking over in December 2011. *El
Cholo*'s work with Atlético had so far proved not merely
transformative but revolutionary. *Colchonero* defender
João Miranda summed up the reasons why Atlético
had just won their second Europa League trophy in
three years – a 3-0 win over Athletic Bilbao in the final
in May 2012: "There's just no comparison between
Manzano and Simeone. We're at least 70% better than
we used to be. I feel like I've been transferred to a
different team."

Costa arrived back in Madrid below par and had to
undergo arthroscopic surgery on his knee. Agüero and

Forlán were no longer around – the former sold to Manchester City and the latter joining Internazionale – but the Brazilian now had to compete for a place in the front line with Radamel Falcao, Adrián, Raúl García and '*Cebolla*' (The Onion) Rodríguez. He also knew that once again the club would have to get rid of a non-EU player. Simeone had decided that either Costa or 'Toto' Salvio would have to go. Costa found himself in precisely the same situation as he had been in 12 months earlier. His road to the first team was blocked. He was a coin toss away from a transfer.

"I wasn't under any illusions, and knew that the easiest thing would be to leave," remembers Costa. "I had a few offers [Betis were interested and Atléti had asked for €5m] and Atlético could certainly have done with the money. It would have been easier to replace me than other players and it would also have freed up a place for a non-EU player. I told my agent that I didn't want to be loaned out again. I wanted a real chance to prove myself, regardless of where that might be. Above all I wanted to stop moving from city to city."

Paulo Assunção had left Atlético to return to Brazil in the summer of 2012, and his former team-mate and compatriot called him for advice. Work hard in pre-season, said the defender. See how the land lies after that, and then make a decision.

Costa's future looked even more bleak, at least in the short term, when the coach took him to one side and told him that the Argentine winger Toto would be his first choice for the final non-EU position.

Simeone: "I told him straight but I also reminded him that things can change and explained that for me he'd be just one more member of my squad training and preparing for the new season. That conversation seemed to light a fire under him. He started to work really hard and it took our breath away."

The key to Costa's reprieve at Atlético, however, had little to do with the player himself. Toto had been loaned to Benfica for most of season 2010-11, and had impressed in Portugal before a calf injury sent him back to Madrid, where he had featured regularly under Simeone during the following season. However, Benfica had not forgotten about him, and now a delegation from the club arrived in Spain to make a bid of €11m for Toto. It was an offer that Atlético could not refuse.

Costa was under no illusion about the key factor in his continued presence on the training pitch as the new season neared. "It's ended up being Toto who has left, but I have no doubt that it would have been me if Benfica hadn't come in with that offer."

Costa did not play in the season opener against Levante, and came off the bench for only the final 20 minutes of the subsequent 4-0 thrashing of Athletic Bilbao. To make matters worse, he saw no game time as Atlético defeated Chelsea, the Champions League holders, 4-1 in Monaco to claim the UEFA Supercup.

Unlike Atlético's previous win in that tournament, when Costa joined in the party as if he had played an integral part in the team's win, this time he was a killjoy. Journalists picked up on the vibe, as did Simeone, the coach who had yet to connect with the wildcard of his striking roster. The next fixture was against Rayo, the club where Costa had caught fire during the second half of the previous season. Simeone identified it as a motivational opportunity and told the Brazilian to show him he had been wrong to ignore him.

Atlético won 4-3 – though they were 4-0 up with eight minutes to play. Costa scored his first goal since returning to Madrid in a 4-2 win at Real Betis at the end of September. Soon his partnership with Falcao was driving an early-season charge and Costa had vaulted to the front of Simeone's forwards.

"Radamel deserves the best," said Costa. "He works harder than anyone else and is a brilliant guy. I've never felt jealous of him. You have to learn from great players and he has taught me so much."

Cries of 'Diego, Diego' – which had been directed at his countryman Diego Ribas during the previous season, when the playmaker was on loan from Wolfsburg – now began to echo around the Calderón in his honour.

By December he had scored in La Liga, the Copa del Rey and the Europa League, but now he started to run up against some familiar demons. On December 2, he picked up his long-standing battle with Pepe and Sergio Ramos during a Madrid derby at the Bernabéu which Simeone's side lost 2-0. There were flashpoints between them throughout, but twice during the match Costa appeared to wipe his nose on his glove and then flick mucus at Ramos.

Four days later he was sent off for a hard foul in a Europa League game against Viktoria Plzen, which Atlético lost 1-0 to finish second in their group. When his young team-mate Pedro Martín, who had just come off the bench, was involved in a confrontation with David Limberský, Costa sprinted over, putting himself between the two players. Limberský collapsed as soon as Costa got in his face, the referee Kristinn Jakobsson saw it as a headbutt and issued a red card.

"It was my fault and I'm sorry," said Costa. "But I do think a red card was a bit much. I didn't headbutt him. He bumped into me when he was getting up. I do accept my share of the blame though and I'm sorry."

Simeone backed his striker at the subsequent press conference. "I love Costa. We believe in him."

In private, the coach told his volatile striker: "All your talents are no use to me if you don't get to use them."

This would not be the last time the coach would have to speak to the player, who was banned for four games by UEFA.

As well as physical confrontations, Costa was still happy to sledge the defenders he was up against. On

January 25, Atlético drew with Betis in the second leg of the Copa del Rey quarter-finals, giving them a 3-1 aggregate win. Costa scored the crucial opening goal, after an error from Antonio Amaya had given him the opportunity.

Amaya claimed that the striker had whispered, "Thanks, stupid," as he had returned to the pitch after celebrating his goal. Atlético once again defended their player, pointing out that Costa had been repeatedly fouled by Amaya during the game.

The Betis defender added a neat summation of his evening with Costa: "You know, it takes a lot of self control not to give that guy a good slap. I would probably have killed him if I hadn't been held back."

"I have no score to settle with anyone," said Costa. "I don't hold grudges. What happens on the pitch stays on the pitch."

He would say that: "I see nothing wrong in deliberately winding-up my opponents. It's just a strategy."

After this turbulent start to 2013, it became clear that Costa was the breakout star of the Atlético squad. The *rojiblancos* visited one of his favourite grounds, El Sadar, on March 17 to face Osasuna, and Costa gave a bravura performance in his 100th match in La Liga. This was the stadium where, during season 2010/11, Costa had scored a hat-trick for Atléti. Osasuna were aggressive, direct and played in front of a hostile support – perfect conditions for Costa; and the striker responded, right up until his ankle gave way.

Costa trotted on to the pitch, laughing and joking with his old friend Alejandro Arribas.

He scored with a quick reaction, heading in from close range after his shot was brilliantly saved by Andrés Fernández. He celebrated by 'shushing' the home fans and pointing to the No.19 and the name on his back. His second goal was pure Diego Costa. He ploughed through one tackle on the left, and then was clattered by a second. His reaction – declining the offer of a handshake and baiting his opponent right in front of the referee – ensured a caution for both Costa and his assailant. Then, with the stadium jeering him, the free-kick came in and Costa muscled himself into position at the back post to tuck away his second goal in a 2-0 win. The Brazilian was on the point of scoring a third goal when he twisted his ankle and had to be substituted by Adrián. The striker dragged himself over to sit on the bench as spittle and assorted missiles rained upon him from the stands.

The Osasuna coach, José Luis Mendilibar – Costa's mentor at Valladolid – told the press: "He's always very difficult to play against. He plays brilliantly and is an enormous asset for the team. I'm sure Simeone is very grateful to him because he's the player who sustains their attack. He may have a certain reputation but Costa has been pulling Atlético's chestnuts out of the fire for a while now."

El Mundo led with "Diego Costa is all they need".

Unexpectedly, Atlético were out of the Europa League after defeat by Rubin Kazan in the first knockout round. Immediately, the defeat was used as motivation to capitalise on their strong position in the two domestic competitions.

Now that Champions League qualification was well in hand, the Atlético supporters had turned their attention to the Copa del Rey. Having dispatched Jaén, Getafe and Betis, Simeone's men met Sevilla in the semi-finals.

A fierce rivalry had recently developed between the two teams and just before kick-off the Sevilla players were treated to a foretaste of what they could expect from Costa. The striker greeted the match officials warmly but then assumed an angry scowl as he walked down the line-up, shaking hands with the opposition.

At the Calderón, Costa scored two penalties in a tense 2-1 victory, winning the first himself. He was also the victim, with five minutes to play, of a vicious foul by Fernando Navarro which resulted in a red card for the Spain international.

Five minutes into the second leg, in Seville's Sánchez Pizjuán stadium, Costa silenced the home support, taking a couple of neat touches on the edge of the box before drilling a low shot into the bottom-left corner. Falcao added another to seal the tie, although Sevilla came back to draw 2-2 on the night with goals from Jesús Navas, then Ivan Rakitić in the final minute.

In the final 15 minutes of the game, Gary Medel, Geoffrey Kondogbia and Juan Carlos Carcedo, the Sevilla assistant coach, had all been shown red cards, with Costa the common factor. First the striker drew Medel into a 50-50 under a high ball and hit the ground when the Chilean barged into him. Then Kondogbia slid through the back of Costa and stood on his groin when getting up. The defender would later claim that he had stamped on Costa in response to constant racist abuse and refused to shake the Brazilian's hand when the teams next met in the league.

It was left to the Sevilla striker Álvaro Negredo to sum up the mood in the Sevilla camp: "Costa set us up and we fell for it."

The Copa del Rey final took place in the Santiago Bernabéu stadium on May 17, 2013, against Real Madrid. Costa would later describe the game as "the most important match of my career".

Asked in the build-up what the difference between the teams was, Simeone said: "€400m per year on the budget." There were other ways to quantify it. Real Madrid had won every one of the 10 previous derbies. Atlético had not beaten their old foes in the 25 matches they had played since returning to La Liga.

This one started in a brutally familiar fashion. Real pinned their opponents back, and Cristiano Ronaldo scored a majestic header, battling free of Diego Godín's clutches at a corner, reading the flight perfectly and heading down into the bottom-left corner at the very top of his jump.

This was Simeone's Atléti, however. Things had changed. Radamel Falcao, isolated and frustrated up front, began to drop deep. Costa, returned to the team in a wide role on the right, started to run beyond his team-mate. It paid off.

In the 34th minute, Falcao wriggled between Raúl Albiol and Sami Khedira near halfway, spun and sent a perfect diagonal pass into the run of Costa. The striker sprinted clear of Fábio Coentrão and, as he entered the box, thumped a low shot across Diego López and in off the post.

The celebrations were so rabid that Arda Turan nearly tore the No.19 shirt off Costa's back. The boy from Lagarto was now the tournament's top goalscorer and had been on target in every round.

Ronaldo had been roughed up by Simeone's men and cracks began to show. First Jose Mourinho was sent off for confronting the referee, Carlos Clos Gomez, after a foul on his ace by Mario Suárez.

Madrid hit the woodwork three times but during an agonising period of extra-time Koke served up a perfect assist to the front post, where Miranda arrived to glance in a subtle header.

Ronaldo followed his manager down the tunnel six minutes from the end of extra-time, after he appeared to flick his boot at Gabi's face after a challenge on him by the Atlético player. Gabi was off soon after that, picking up a second yellow for encroachment as his team killed the clock. The minutes become seconds. The whistle brought bedlam.

Spain's capital was *Colchonero*. The jinx was over. Atlético had won their fourth final in enemy territory, their 10th Copa del Rey, the third trophy in less than a year and a half under Simeone.

'Atlético – Kings of the Bernabéu', declared the headlines.

Inside the dressing room, the pictures of Saint Gema and Saint Ildefonso had assumed the status of lucky amulets for the newly crowned champions. The club president, Enrique Cerezo, enveloped Costa in a delighted hug whilst at the back of the room Arda Turan was sticking to a pre-match promise and shaving his head.

"This is the worst season of my life," said Mourinho. "A Super Cup, a semi-final, a runner-up. For many coaches that would be a good year. For me it is the worst."

For Atléti, it was one of the best. The celebrations continued the following day and Costa led the way from the top of the bus taking the team to the Neptune statue and fountain in the middle of Madrid, where Atléti traditionally celebrate their trophies.

"The players never stopped believing," said Simeone to the raucous crowd. "For 14 years we could not win, but we had the strength to wait until it happened. We won the best match. We won the final. We won in the Bernabéu."

With third place in La Liga – and qualification for the Champions League – secured, Costa and Atlético could look forward to the pursuit of still more silverware at home and abroad next season.

PARTIDO A PARTIDO

*'The charge of a conquering army is like the bursting of
pent waters into a chasm a thousand fathoms deep'*

Sun Tzu, *The Art of War*

DIEGO COSTA WAS granted Spanish nationality
in the summer of 2013 and on July 5 the striker
presented himself at the Civil Registry in Madrid to
swear allegiance to the Spanish constitution. Now, at
last, Atlético had one more space for a non-EU player.
This was great news for the club but Costa's new status
also made him an attractive proposition for any club
shopping for a striker in the summer transfer market.

Liverpool were quickest off the mark, offering €25m
for the Brazilian and triggering the release clause in his
contract. However, Jose Mourinho, recently returned to
Chelsea, had also identified Costa as a primary target,
a Didier Drogba-style centre-forward around whom he
could forge a new winning machine. The Portuguese
coach had watched Costa since he first arrived at Braga,
and had felt the force of the striker during his breakout
season close-up as manager of Real Madrid.

However, Mourinho had yet to persuade the owner
of Chelsea, Roman Abrahmovich, to accelerate his
rebuilding plans. In both acquiring new players and

moving others on, the process would be gradual. For example, Benfica's Nemanja Matić, another immediate target for the new manager, would have to wait until January 2014.

If Costa could not be signed now, a strategy was needed to ensure he was delayed, and not diverted. Chelsea and Mourinho made their case to Costa and Atlético: turn down Liverpool now and we will sign you – for more money – in 12 months. Samuel Eto'o was the stop-gap acquisition. Behind the scenes, Costa was lined up for summer 2014, in negotiations aimed at making all parties happy for the season ahead. On August 14, the club renewed Costa's contract, doubling the salary and extending until June 2018. The release clause also went up, and the understanding was that the new season would be Costa's last for *Los Colchoneros*.

For Atléti, the sale could wait. At the start of pre-season, Falcao packed his bags and moved to Monaco for a fee reported at €60m. In came David Villa from Barcelona for €5.1m. Business was good, but Costa now carried a weight of responsibility for Simeone. A player who so often had been a whisker away from a bargain-basement transfer out of Atléti was now one of the crown jewels of the team.

"I'd like to thank the club for offering me an extended contract. I hope to do even better so that I can help the team achieve everything we have set out to do," Costa declared. The club's sports director, José Luis Pérez

Caminero, said: "This is great news for us all. Diego is a vital part of this team and it was a priority to extend his contract. We want to continue to move forward with the same group of players who have brought us so much success over the last few years."

"After everything I've gone through to make it to the first team here, how could I leave now?" Costa asked.

Costa would take another quantum leap forward in 2013-2014 and Simeone's Atléti would reach heights few imagined they were capable of.

Atlético's season kicked off in Sevilla, the scene of the crime, as far as Costa was concerned.

"We can't force Costa to change the person that he is," insisted Simeone before the game, when the spectre of the Copa matches was raised. Costa scored twice in a 3-1 away win which was a statement of intent for his team.

Next came defeat on away goals after two draws in the Supercup series against Barcelona. In the closing stages of the 0-0 second-leg, both Arda Turan and Filipe Luís were sent off.

After that, however, Simeone's side exploded into their best-ever start to a season, and Costa was slamming in goals – seven in the first six games.

Matchday seven in La Liga saw the Madrid derby and Atlético once again triumphed at the Bernabéu. The only goal of the match came from Costa. Koke, as usual, laid on the silver-service pass. Costa, one-on-one with Diego López, slid it home. He ran to the corner, fingers to his lips in what was becoming a trademark celebration. There was still time to go at it with Ramos and Pepe – all three would end up with yellow cards.

"Calm down, we need you," pleaded his team-mates, watching him go nose-to-nose with referee Mateu Lahoz, who was remonstrating with the Brazilian for his constant brawling. As astute as ever, Simeone decided to bring Costa off and the Bernabéu echoed to the sound of whistles and jeers as he left the pitch – indisputable proof that Costa had earned the respect of the enemy support. His goals had earned Atlético two historic victories, back-to-back wins at the Bernabéu for the first time since the 1920-1921 season.

"Diego Costa makes the Bernabéu his own", trumpeted the headlines.

Two more goals followed on October 6 against Celta de Vigo, making Costa La Liga's top scorer and taking Atlético's streak to eight wins from eight.

"A complete striker who looks unstoppable," wrote Ladislao J. Moñino in *El País*.

The streak was broken by Espanyol at Cornellá-El Prat. The Champions League was next.

Two days after losing to Espanyol, Atlético beat Zenit, and without Costa, who had two matches remaining on the ban he picked up in the Czech Republic. He missed the subsequent win over Porto, too, and so would make his Champions League debut in Vienna's Ernst Happel stadium, where the Austrian champions Austria Vienna awaited.

"My team-mates always told me that playing in the Champions League was something else. A totally unique sensation," Costa said. "It always made me want to experience it for myself. It's like a dream come true for any footballer, having the chance to play and score in this competition."

No sooner said than done. Raúl García stuck away the first after eight minutes. Twelve minutes later Costa picked the ball up around halfway and set off on a Ronaldinho-esque gallop towards the goal, dancing around Manuel Ortlechner before finishing with power past Heinz Linder. After the break he picked up a fox-in-the-box goal to leave Austria with three away points and a feeling that there really wasn't much to this Champions League stuff. When Austria Vienna came to Madrid for the reverse fixture on the following matchday, Costa missed a penalty but scored the last in a 4-0 rout.

Simeone continued to work his miracles in the league. Atléti won eight of the nine games following their defeat by Espanyol, including a 7-0 win over Getafe. Costa started on the bench that day, but came on to score a further two goals, one a superb overhead kick.

"Diego is a giant, in every sense of the word," said the coach on November 4, after a victory against Athletic Bilbao. "He's learning how to support other players, to win the ball back more and how to connect with the rest of his team. And that helps the whole team perform better. Really, the sky's the limit for this guy."

His fellow striker, David Villa, agreed. "I love playing with him. He scores goals, works hard for the team and is strong and very tough."

By the winter of 2013 Costa was the man of the moment in Spanish football. Koke had provided assists for two thirds of his goals and the two men had developed a highly effective partnership. They would often stay late at training to discuss how to find each other on the pitch.

After a 3-2 win over Levante on December 21, Simeone said: "If they extended the voting period for the Balon d'Or, Diego Costa would be a strong contender."

The striker had 19 goals from 17 matches as 2013 ended, amid talk of a title push from Atléti, and from Simeone, over and over, talk of taking it *partido a partido* – one game at a time. The Argentine would turn a banal football cliché into a mantra for a remarkable season.

Costa's arrival amongst the elite was confirmed when journalist Jesús Gallego decided to write a song in homage to the player. Based on Joaquin Sabina's *Qué demasiao* [Too Much] and with a bit of musical help from Pancho Varona and his guitar, the tribute went something like this:

He's the gangster wearing red and white
Scoring goals
Ready for the fight
A sure fire killer wearing football boots
Diego Costa aims and shoots
So many reasons why
We're crazy 'bout this guy

There, in the Calderón
They cheer their favourite son
Gives defenders what he gets
Then slams the ball into the net
With our backs against the wall
It's Diego on the ball
Getting in their face
Cos man, he rules this space

If the bastards go in hard
Then Diego's just as bad
Kicking ass, he's in the zone
And then he thumps it home

Back in Sergipe, Brazil, another duo, Chiko Queiroga and Antônio Rogério, decided to dedicate a song to Costa, which was an instant success on social networks. The striker's popularity had reached a new high and every weekend the Calderón stadium would reverberate to the ever-more enthusiastic chants of 'Diego Costa oé, oé'.

With the start of 2014, old doubts began to surface. How soon would the team run out of steam? Could the players, so carefully looked after by Óscar 'The Professor' Ortega, Simeone's fitness coach, keep up the pace?

They emerged from their first game of the year against Málaga with a 1-0 victory, courtesy of a Koke goal. Manchester United's head scout Robbie Cooke was in attendance at La Roselada that day, yet more evidence of the fact that Costa had become one of the most admired strikers in Europe. But Manchester United was not the only English club watching the player.

In January, Atlético drew with Sevilla in the Calderón, where Federico Fazio emerged as a personal nemesis for Costa. During an intense personal duel, Costa shoved the defender in the face and the Argentine responded with a big punch to the striker's stomach. If that was a stumble, the *Rojiblanco* backfired in February. Defeats away to Almeria and Osasuna raised doubts over the ability to go the distance in La Liga. Home and away losses to Madrid in the Copa del Rey – a 5-0 aggregate defeat – hurt more and gave one of their title rivals a psychological edge.

Aside from that mini-slump, however, there was a prestigious win over Athletic Bilbao in the newly finished San Mamés stadium. Atlético were first-footing the new stadium and Costa gave an outstanding performance on the rain-soaked pitch, scoring the equaliser in a 2-1 come-from-behind win.

Now a Champions League last-16 tie with Milan beckoned. "He's like a PlayStation player," said Koke of his foil as he trotted on to the San Siro pitch to train. This would be Simeone's Atlético's first experience in one of the great cathedrals of European football, which was perhaps a factor in the poor quality of football they produced in the first 45 minutes against a masterful Milan. However, just when it looked like both sides would settle for 0-0, Costa headed the ball past Christian Abbiati.

"Saint Diego conquers the San Siro," declared Spanish newspaper Marca with a grandiose flourish. The Italian press was more pragmatic, leading with: "Diego Costa makes them pay."

"Just like the great Italian teams of the past, this Atlético is based on a great goalkeeper [Courtois] and an elite striker," argued *Gazzetta dello Sport*, the day after the win.

Many expected the glorious result to be repeated in the Calderón, but before Atléti could think about the return leg against Milan, they had to face an excruciating derby against Real Madrid. So intense and closely fought was the encounter, which ended in a 2-2 draw, that during the official presentation of his new boots, Costa made an interesting (and very typical) comment:

"If I have to give Sergio Ramos a kick, then so be it. And he likewise will kick me if he has to. But it's about competition. It's only when we're playing."

The two players would both later use the word 'brothers' to describe their relationship, thereby encapsulating what was becoming one of the most productive and mutually respectful personal rivalries in Spanish football.

The visit of Milan in the second leg of the last-16 of the Champions League was a pivotal match in the season. Atléti, we learned, were now capable of bringing one of the great European clubs to its knees – and all this after an early goal from Kaká had cancelled out Costa's own strike in the first leg.

Atlético responded with four goals in a devastating show of strength. There were two more for Costa. After his first, a wonderfully controlled back-post volley, he put both gloved hands over his eyes, a reminder, as he had promised, to those criticising his intentions to represent Spain that he was blind to their opinions. That goal came after 158 seconds, Atléti's fastest in the elite European competition. It meant seven in Costa's first five Champions League matches – the best start of any player in the history of the tournament.

At the end of the match Costa swapped shirts with Mario Balotelli, with whom he had had a bruising encounter in the away leg. "Diego Costa has demonstrated that he is a champion who plays for his team, whilst Balotelli is a player who plays for himself," concluded the Italian journalist Alberto Cerrutti. "We already knew that Atlético Madrid were amongst the top eight in Europe but now, more importantly, we know that they have a good chance of winning the European Cup," concluded the Cadena COPE journalist Paco González.

"Diego can still get even better," Simeone told a group of US journalists after the game. "He is immensely strong, both in physical and psychological terms and there's no doubt that he can still improve as a player. This guy is destined for great things, but he brings a sense of humility to everything he does. Nothing has been handed to him on a plate. He has enormous intelligence and talent, but his success is a result of his drive and hard work. He has raised the quality of the whole team and we are hugely proud of his development here."

El Cholo's words of praise for his *Bestia* (Beast) were backed up by the stats. The Brazilian had the highest precision in the league (almost 71% of his shots at goal hit the target) and more opponents were booked for challenges on him than either Messi or Ronaldo.

Costa was a thorn in the side of La Liga defences everywhere, and not just because of his goals. Jorge Valdano, the former sporting director of Real Madrid and a World Cup winner, would call him "a defender playing up front". "I have never seen a striker kick people so much," complained the Argentine.

The week after Atléti hammered Milan, Costa dedicated his winner against Espanyol to his Lagarto friend, Emerson Daniel Souza, who had died in a traffic accident, lifting his shirt to show a vest bearing the words 'Eterno Totoca'.

In the press, Costa was hailed as the cyclone that was keeping Atlético's hopes alive in its romantic assault on the habitual big beasts of La Liga. Costa, the hyperactive star, was their greatest ally in that push. The *Ecos del Balón* declared: "We need to separate the wheat from the chaff and recognise that it is Costa and Courtois who are bringing this team so much success," underneath the headline: 'Diegaut Coustois does it again'.

Atlético consolidated their position at the top of the league by defeating Granada and then Betis. Suddenly the impossible looked entirely possible.

Against Betis, Costa had another of the physical contests which marked his best work. "He's like your typical Sunday-morning footballer who turns up with three aims: he wants a game, he wants to score and he wants a bit of a fight," concluded José Antonio Martín Otín 'Petón', an agent and writer who was an unofficial spokesman for this Atlético group.

On this occasion Costa was up against his countryman, Paulão. First the striker pushed the defender into a touchline fence, then the defender gave Costa a good booting. "Come on. You and me" signaled the Betis player, pointing aggressively at Costa. Then, within minutes, as the final whistle sounded on a 2-0 win for Atléti in which Costa scored once, the two players laughed happily as they high-fived each other.

Atlético remained top, a fact emphasised by a superb performance which once more silenced the San Mamés. Atléti came back from a goal down once more against Athletic Bilbao, with Koke and Costa scoring in a 2-1 win. The headline in *As,* March 30: 'The Basque home hosts another Diego Costa exhibition.'

"Atléti competes, Costa destroys", wrote journalist José Miguélez. Iñako Díaz-Guerra's match report in *As* said: "An epic hero in a performance which was powerful enough to be called incredible: Diego Costa – a thousand sprints, hundreds of little details, a goal and then off the pitch exhausted after a supernatural effort. Diego Costa is the great leader."

"Diego Costa could invade an average-sized country all by himself," tweeted journalist Santi Giménez.

In the last 31 games in which Costa had scored, Atlético had won the match.

Óscar Ortega, 'The Prof' behind the immense conditioning of Simeone's team, had never seen anything like the striker. He said: "Diego Costa's physical strength defies logic. He's like a bull. He has certain qualities that you just can't explain, no matter how much you've studied. It's totally illogical that he could go to Rayo and score nine goals when he was still recovering from a serious injury and had done no real preparatory work. I was blown away when I saw him that first season. I asked him about his youth-team experience and he told me that he didn't have any, that he'd learned his football on the streets. There are no limits to this guy's strength."

In the Cerro del Espino training sessions Costa was now a central figure. His transformation was complete and his importance to the team that was the talk of world football drove him to improve still further. "I like to make a difference and love that when people see me on the pitch they think, 'Everything will be fine. We've got Diego,'" the player said.

"Right now the fans see Simeone and Diego Costa as the driving power behind the team," said Jesús García Pitarch, the former director of football.

"I have a theory," García Pitarch continues. "Costa always had the potential to become a great player but he lacked 300 games. That's the number of games your average 18-year-old La Liga footballer would have already played at youth level. Diego's problem was that he had never been in an organised team and had no experience of the dressing room, of being part of a team. He lacked any sense of discipline, of belonging to a club. He was already 15 or 16 before his football took off and he lacked the experience that would have helped him realise his potential. If things had been different there's no doubt that he would have exploded on to the scene much earlier – in 2009 rather than in 2011. He's also had a lot of bad luck along the way. For example, after performing so well at Penafiel, he was on the point of playing for Braga when he broke a finger. And then there was his knee injury. He's had an uphill struggle. He missed 40 games because of those injuries and you can add that number to the 300 matches he missed out on as a youngster. He was always going to be great, it was just going to take him a bit longer than other people.

"Diego had to go through all of that to get where he is today. He needed to compete, to play lots of games. He needed all those bookings, the red cards, the fury, the dives, the spitting – you need to make mistakes, you need to learn, you need to go through the wringer. He's had the trajectory he required in order to distinguish for himself the difference between real intensity and getting into rows all the time or bad sportsmanship. He needed to make the mistakes. He needed to play the games."

"He's reinvented himself to a very great extent," says Javier Hernández, the man who first spotted Costa's potential. "Other players go out on loan and lose their foothold, but he used those experiences to grow up and mature. He deserves huge credit for the speed at which he has taken on and applied concepts that were completely new to him. I wouldn't change him for the world. I love a player with his level of aggression and you see less and less of them nowadays. Any coach in the world would give his right arm for a player like Diego who can put any back four in the world in difficulties."

"I think I've gone about things the right way," said the player himself. "I got lots of playing time when I was out on loan and used that to familiarise myself with the league and correct and improve my game. I always believed that if I continued to learn then I could be a success at Atlético. I've changed a lot. I used to struggle to accept certain things and my attitude was completely different. Now things have changed and I'm fighting to be an important part of a great club. I have had difficult moments in my career but it has all been good for me. I've grown up a lot and I don't regret a thing. I've learned something from every experience. And that's why I am where I am today."

"He was very pig-headed, very determined. 'I'll be playing here one day,' he used to say in the dressing room," recalls Juan Valera, who was a team-mate at Atléti when Costa arrived, but had moved out to Getafe by the time he made his breakthrough. "Then our teams were in the same train one day and he said, 'Told you so. I told you I'd end up in the team'. But then football can be like that. Sometimes you have to be in the right place at the right time. He definitely deserves all his success."

"People have no idea how hard life can be for players," says Paulo Assunção, who watched the final stages of Costa's rise from Brazil, playing for São Paulo.

"Diego came from nowhere and he's made it to the top through sheer hard graft. He's learning more with every year. He could end up being considered on a par with Messi and Cristiano."

"He wins games single handed and has made a huge difference to Atléti," said Bernardo Salazar, who wrote the history of the *Colchoneros*. "If Diego continues like this he will end up as one of the greatest strikers Atléti has ever had."

As Atlético turned the corner and prepared for the home stretch in a season that would go down in their history, Simeone reflected on the nature of his No.19. "Costa is a marvel. He's unique. He's a rebel. He's capable of winning the Balon d'Or."

Costa had been outstanding so far, in what was proving the most demanding season of his career but the next 60 days would bring a new kind of pressure and Costa would pay a high price as the physical and emotional demands reached new heights. He was going to learn that his body, battered and bruised after so many battles on the pitch, could only be pushed so far.

Arguably, the Athletic Bilbao game at the end of March was Costa's last great performance of season 2013-14. As the finishing tape neared in the punishing races for titles in La Liga and the Champions League, it became clear that he was struggling. The normally armour-plated Brazilian began to look vulnerable and at times it seemed that he was surviving on sheer willpower alone.

In early April, Atlético played the away game of the Champions League quarter-finals at the Camp Nou and Costa managed just 30 minutes on the pitch. He almost certainly should have been withdrawn even sooner. Costa tried to carry a hamstring injury that was apparent to anyone watching the game, including his manager. The striker begged Simeone not to take him off, and the coach prevaricated before making the call. Diego replaced him, and Costa watched from the bench as the substitute's spectacular, long-range goal opened the scoring. Neymar equalised for Barcelona.

"Diego Costa didn't want to leave the field," said Simeone after the game. "The injury he received wasn't the one he had before – he received so many knocks it's difficult to know where it came from."

As the tie headed to the Calderón, it was firmly in Atlético's favour, even if their warrior centre-forward was now being patched up from game to game. The injury he had tried to ignore would keep him out for 10 days.

He missed the next two games on doctors' orders, and both were tough encounters. On April 5 Atlético just managed to scrape a win against Villarreal in the Calderón with a goal from Raúl García. Then, four days later, the *Colchoneros*, with Adrián deputising for Costa, knocked Barcelona out of the Champions

League with a 1-0 win in the return leg in front of a rapturous crowd, scoring early through Koke and giving nothing away. It was a vindication for Simeone, who had withstood Costa's petition to play.

Simeone: "For the return leg I had to take an important decision: play Diego Costa – who had just recovered from an injury – or not. I decided he shouldn't play, nor even sit on the bench, because I thought that if we had to play with Costa against Barça then lose him in progressing, it would mean we couldn't have him in the league, which would be unfair for a team that had already worked hard to win that competition.

"I spoke with Costa, and to begin with he understood. I said 'We'll watch how things progress before the game'. When I realised he wasn't in the condition I thought he should be in, he got angry and came to me to say 'Boss, I'm fit to play'. We spoke and arrived at the understanding that I didn't consider him to be in the best state, and that if we were going to go through to the next round, we would do it with him or without him. And that's how it was, because I believe in teams, not individuals."

It was not the last time the two men would have this kind of conversation.

Costa returned to the team on April 13 for a match against Getafe in the Coliseum Alfonso Pérez Stadium. With five minutes to play, the score is 1-0 to Atlético, and Costa has seen his weak penalty saved. Then Adrián tucks a low pass across goal and the striker barrels in at full speed toward the back post. He slides in hard, stabbing the ball into the net and then colliding violently with the upright. Costa howls in agony. Filipe takes one look at the deep cut on Costa's leg and calls for the medics. After much panic on the bench, it is clear that there is no fracture. Costa's goal has ensured another step on the way to the championship, but his body has sustained yet more damage.

The club are quick to ease the fears of their fans. On Twitter, Atlético post: "Luckily, Diego Costa only has a wound after hitting the post."

Simeone adds at the post-match press conference: "He is happy and well. One more cut does not do anything to this tiger."

Even the coach's praise of his striker has to acknowledge the punishment he is enduring as the matches pile up.

The injured leg heavily bandaged, Costa is back in the team for the following match. He scores an injury-time penalty to help his team to a 2-0 win against Elche. It is his 27th and final goal in La Liga.

Atlético's attention had now turned to the Champions League semi-final against Chelsea.

By now, the transfer of Costa to Chelsea in the summer of 2014 was being reported openly. In Mourinho's first season back, his team had been weakened by the lack of goals from its strikers: Samuel

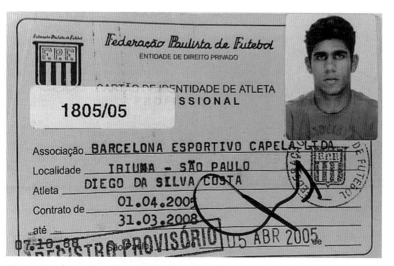

Diego Costa's membership card for Barcelona Esportivo Capela de Ibiúna in São Paulo.

Standing before the veritable shrine to Diego at the family home in Lagarto stand (from left to right) his brother Jair, his father José, his mother Josileide and his sister Talita.

Right: Costa challenges his friend, Paulo Assunção, while playing for Braga against Porto during his first season in Europe.

Left: July 10, 2007, Costa poses for his first photoshoot in the famous red and white stripes of Atlético Madrid.

Left: Costa in action for Celta Vigo.

From Celta Vigo, Costa moved to Albacete, where he became one of the best strikers in the second division.

Right: On loan again, now at Valladolid, his prolific goal scoring could not prevent the side's relegation from the *Primera*.

Left: After nearly six months out with a serious knee injury, Costa returned to action with a bang, scoring for Vallecano in the Romareda against Zaragoza.

Right: Costa and Sergio Ramos clash as Rayo Vallecano take on Real Madrid at Vallecas, their first encounter in what would become a fierce rivalry.

Left: Finally playing in the Atlético colours, Costa and Diego Forlan celebrate his first goal for the club, scored against Zaragoza, on 26 September 2010 .

Right: Costa roars in delight after scoring the goal that sparked Atlético's comeback against Real Madrid at the Bernabeu that would secure the 2013 Copa del Rey.

Costa celebrates with fellow goal scorer Miranda after the 2-1 win in the Copa del Ray.

Costa makes his Brazil debut on 21 March 2013 against Italy in Geneva.

Right: Costa with Vicente del Bosque, the Spain coach who convinced him to change his international allegiance.

Costa makes his debut as a starter for Spain against Italy on 5 March, 2014.

Diego Simeone celebrates with his star player.

Left: Costa silences the crowd in the San Siro with a goal that set Atlético on the road to the quarter finals of the 2013/14 Champions League.

By securing a draw against Barcelona at Camp Nou in the last league game of the season, *Los Colchoneros* were crowned 2013/14 La Liga champions.

Costa scores from the penalty spot during the Champions League semi-final second leg match against Chelsea – who he would join the following season.

After lasting barely nine minutes because of his hamstring problems, Costa is forced out of the Champions League final. Real Madrid would go on to seal 'La Decima' in his absence, winning 4-1.

Costa's official 2014 World Cup portrait. The tournament would prove to be an unhappy return to the country of his birth.

Costa and his Spanish teammates (from left to right, David Silva, Costa, Sergio Busquets, Andres Iniesta and Xabi Alonso) cast dejected figures in the wake of their 2-0 loss to Group B rivals Chile, which confirmed the defending champions' exit from the World Cup.

Costa marks his league debut for Chelsea with a goal against Burnley at Turf Moor. It was his first strike in a whirlwind start to his Premier League career.

The win against Everton at Goodison Park in August 2014 was the perfect introduction to Diego Costa for those in England who had never seen him before: two goals, a yellow card and a series of confrontations.

Costa quickly developed an almost telepathic understanding at Chelsea with his Spanish teammate Cesc Fàbregas. The duo would combine brilliantly throughout the course of the 2014/15 campaign.

Jose Mourinho congratulates the man dubbed by many as 'the new Drogba'.

Cup final goalscorers: Costa and John Terry celebrate with the League Cup, Costa's first trophy in England, after defeating Tottenham Hotspur 2-0 at Wembley Stadium on March 1, 2015.

Costa clashes with former Chelsea defender, David Luiz, in the second leg of the Champions League Round of 16, against PSG at Stamford Bridge. The Parisians would progress to the quarter finals on away goals.

Costa celebrates with the Premier League trophy after defeating Sunderland at
Stamford Bridge on May 24, 2015.

Eto'o, Fernando Torres and Demba Ba. Costa was a solution in waiting. Even Simeone accepted that a deal was on the cards. "It will depend on him and what he thinks is best for his future," said the coach. "We understand that Chelsea have huge financial power and if he wants to live off football for the rest of his life, I will have no problem in him going. Samuel Eto'o has made them better and Diego Costa could do his thing there, but for now he is ours."

The business side of the tie was almost as engrossing as the football aspect. While Simeone was realistic about possible sales, and Atlético remained deep in debt, sporting director José Luis Caminero was still aware that his club held valuable assets and that they had a recent history as strong sellers in the transfer market. He was gearing up for hard ball with Chelsea, on and off the pitch. "Last year we wanted to consolidate the group of players that we currently have and we renewed the contracts of pretty much all of them, including Diego Costa," he said. "Our minds are set on keeping this group of players together and steadily bring in one or two more, who can reinforce what we're doing with our project. We want all our big players to stay and we're planning for next season with them."

In tandem with their transparent pursuit of Costa – and perhaps an influence in these negotiations – Chelsea were also deciding whether or not to try to block the participation of Thibaut Courtois, the goalkeeper they had loaned to Atlético and who had become one of their most influential players, and were also weighing up a move for the left-back Filipe Luís. For their part, Atlético were considering a repatriation of their former icon Fernando Torres. All four players would play their part in what was to come.

The first leg in the Calderón ended in a 0-0 draw. Costa spent most of the match surrounded by Gary Cahill, John Terry and David Luiz and was unable to make any real impact on the game.

Between the Champions League ties, Atlético scored what looked like a huge win over Valencia at the Mestalla, Raúl García's goal all the league leaders needed. Costa put another 90 minutes on his clock for the season.

As a result of that victory in a match their rivals hoped they would drop points, Atlético arrived in London with confidence – and with Costa. They were 90 minutes away from the second European Cup final in their history.

Torres opens the scoring in the 36th minute, his low shot taking a slight deflection on its way past Courtois, the goalkeeper playing against his parent club. Adrián scores the equaliser just before half-time, firing a cut-back into the ground and up into the net. The advantage tie has flip-flopped back to Simeone's team.

In the second half, behind on the away goals rule, Mourinho begins to take risks, and the game opens up. Costa reads the flight of a high ball into the box and nudges it away from Samuel Eto'o as the Chelsea striker approaches, drawing the contact and winning the penalty.

There is a huge delay before Costa takes the spot-kick. He is confronted by Ramires and Branislav Ivanović. He cannot get the ball to sit on the spot. He is cautioned by the referee for time wasting. All this before a penalty which could put his team into the final of the Champions League, against the club he will be with next season. At the whistle, he shoots high and straight to give his team the lead. It's an example of the courage Simeone's players have shown all night, all season. As the coach puts it afterwards: "I want to thank the mothers of these players, because they gave them big *cojones* to play the way they did."

Arda Turan scores the killer third, but Costa does not join in the celebrations, as he is grounded after contesting a header in the build-up. It is an increasingly frequent motif. As *Los Colchoneros* celebrate at Stamford Bridge, the home fans cheer themselves up by singing 'Diego Costa, we'll see you next year'.

Atlético's hangover is a miserable 2-0 defeat away to Levante. There are now two league matches to play, and a win at home to Málaga will make the title a formality. However, they are without Costa, and a spectacular save by Willy Caballero from Adrián in the fourth minute of added time keeps it at 1-1 and piles the pressure on

Simeone's team for the final league fixture – a trip to the Camp Nou to take on Barcelona.

The captain faced the media afterwards. "We still believe in this team," said Gabi. "We're going to go there to win. We're used to playing in finals."

A win would have allowed Simeone to rest key players and relieved much of the emotional pressure on his men. Instead, he needed everyone at maximum intensity for back-to-back matches against the two giants of Spanish football – Barcelona and, in the final of the Champions League, Real Madrid.

May 17, 2014. It has been 18 years since Atlético last won the league title.

"We had two finals ahead of us," recalls Koke. "It had been a great season, very long but enjoyable and we all knew that the Barcelona game would be special."

Over in Barcelona the players were just as fired up. Barely a month had passed since the death of Tito Vilanova, their former coach, from cancer. On the pitch, they had endured heavy criticism for a marked dip in form. Despite all of this, Tata Martino's team could win the title with victory in front of their own supporters.

Costa lasts 16 minutes. In a bid to support an attack down the left he attempts a sprint and immediately pulls out. It is a recurrence of the hamstring injury that has curtailed his participation in the final weeks of the season. He hobbles to the bench and covers his tears with his jersey.

Minutes later, Arda Turan joins him, after a freak contact with Cesc Fàbregas injures his hip. Simeone has used two substitutes – and lost two starters – in the first 23 minutes. Ten minutes later, things look even worse. Fàbregas whips a pass in to Leo Messi, whose lay off is hammered in high at the near post of Courtois by Alexis Sánchez.

Courtois: "If you lose two players and they make it 1-0 it's hard for the team and I think half-time came at a good moment."

With Barcelona in the driving seat, Simeone addressed his players at half-time with an inspiring certainty. "If we score we'll be league champions, and you're going to score," the coach told his men again and again.

Next Costa and Arda, both of them still in pain, got to their feet: "Come on lads. You can do it. Do it for us!"

Those words were still ringing in the ears of the players when, three minutes after the restart, Diego Godín rose majestically and powered a fantastic header past Pinto to make it 1-1. Atlético had a winning position and in season 2013-14 there was no team better at closing out a result in that situation.

At the end, as the Barcelona fans cheered the new champions with chants of 'Atléti! Atléti!' Costa came back onto the pitch, all smiles, his red training top over the yellow away shirt, black leggings over his shorts. He joined in the crowd of players who threw Simeone into the air, and then was first to embrace his coach in a big hug. But as he walked round the perimeter of the Camp Nou, he was limping heavily.

"I don't remember him from the post-match party," says *Marca* journalist Alberto Romero Barbero. "He was enjoying himself with everyone else, but you could see that he was thinking about the final in Lisbon the minute that match ended."

The day after winning the league, Costa began his frenetic efforts to get back to full fitness for the Champions League final, seven days later. On Twitter, the club announced that the player suffered a Grade 1 tear of his hamstring. The first prognosis suggested the striker needed a 10-day rest. It may as well have been 100.

Two days after winning the league, Simeone was fielding questions about his injured players. How fit where they? How fit would they have to be to play?

"We will work to have Diego Costa available on Saturday, but it's really difficult," he said. "He is an important player but he needs to be ready. We still have some days to go, we are not going to say anything yet. It is too soon, ahead of an important game. We will prepare in our own way, wait on the injury news from Costa and Arda until the end of the week, and if necessary look for alternatives as needed. This is not a game for players at 80 per cent."

Then a new name entered discussions about Costa's hamstring: Marijana Kovacević. A Serbian doctor who had worked with the Jorge Mendes camp before, Kovacević at first seemed like a provider of a second opinion – a fairly standard route to go down. Until, that is, it emerged that she had a quirky speciality, which was the reason she had been connected to Costa. The striker was to travel to Belgrade to be injected with horse placenta.

The medical staff at Atlético, perhaps unsurprisingly, thought a line had been crossed. Their work had been bypassed in order that the injured player could travel across Europe to be seen by someone they thought was little more than a quack. What was more, some on the staff were concerned about exposing their player to any outside treatment that had the potential of leading to a positive doping test.

Costa set off for Belgrade with Óscar Pitillas, the fitness and recuperation coach who had played such a vital role in his recovery from the ACL injury and who could provide Atlético with some influence in this caper. Not long after arriving, and hearing the details of the treatment, both Costa and Pitillas decided against proceeding. He refused the placenta injections, and after a couple of treatments of a more conventional nature, they returned.

Getting off the plane, Costa and Pitillas were met by a solitary photographer from *Marca*. After the coach had blocked the front-page shot of Costa back on Spanish soil following his supposed miracle cure, the snapper plucked up the courage to ask the striker to come back and pose for a picture. Alberto Romero Barbero of *Marca* remembers that: "Diego was brilliant about it and did what he was asked with good humour – pretty unusual behaviour for an elite footballer. But he was really high that day. He was convinced he'd make it to Lisbon."

In the days following Costa's trip to Serbia, the striker's fitness was the big story in the coverage of the coming final – a situation only amplified by the shroud of secrecy Atlético attempted to throw over the issue.

Javier Amaro, of Radio Marca, was one of several journalists trying to get in front of the Costa story as the final loomed. "Although some people still deny it, Diego came back with a micro-tear which had been diagnosed in the CEMTRO Clinic in Madrid," explains Javier Amaro. "Those same specialists told Simeone that Costa could not play – the risk of further damage was too great. Despite this, Atlético mounted a military operation in their attempts to maintain secrecy at the teams's training ground, Los Ángeles de San Rafael. They even hired a bus for journalists to prevent us from driving our own cars into the ground and there were three police checks to ensure that only authorised personnel got in. They would only allow us to see 15 minutes of training, during which Diego played and all the players told us how much better he was as they left the ground. But all my own sources were still telling me that it would be impossible for him to play in Lisbon."

The confusion caused by all the secrecy resulted in a host of rumours about Costa's state of fitness. David Medina, of *Marca*, received a message from Costa saying he would play in the final – but miss the World Cup as a result. Vicente del Bosque, the Spain coach, was understandably concerned. "It is normal that a player wants to be there, because it is not just another game but the European Cup final," he said. "But he cannot go against his own health. His team, Atlético, and the player himself are those who have to weigh up the situation and the consequences."

Right up until the day of the final, May 24, with the streets of Lisbon overrun by Spaniards, there was still no clarity about whether Costa would play.

The day before, Atlético's training produced a scenario that typified the uncertainty. Costa got through what observers thought to be a brutal session. However, during a sprints session overseen by Pitillas, the trainer had concerns that Costa's running style was unnatural, that he was saving the injured leg. He asked the player if he felt okay, and of course Costa replied in the affirmative. Simeone asked Pitillas to make a call, and the trainer said Costa was not fit to play. The striker, however, was vehement.

Simeone told Costa that he would sleep on his

decision. If it was a heart-versus-head decision, then it was the emotional side of the coach, and not the rational, which prevailed. The coach allowed all that Costa had achieved, all of the points he had won for the team, and his fearsome desire to play, to outweigh the justified concerns over the state of his hamstring. It was a decision he would later recognise as a huge mistake.

Simeone: "Starting Diego Costa or leaving him on the bench was the most difficult decision I've faced as a coach, because the day before in training, there was a huge amount of focus on us. The people who came to watch us saw how he ran 50-metre sprints in the middle of the pitch, participated in possession work, headers, marking... signs that made you think, 'OK, we're playing a Champions league final'.

"In that situation, Diego Costa is such a difference maker, so important for the group, for opponents. Watching him train, I debated between having him on the bench then bringing him on – where he could go on to injure himself – or putting him in the starting line up, having seen what I saw in training and feeling that he could give us 45 good minutes."

Costa warmed up with the rest of the team before the game. Initially he was wearing a bandage, but he removed it and handed it to a member of the coaching staff. Óscar Pitillas remained sceptical about Costa's fitness and called over to Adrián – the player who had replaced the Brazilian when injured – with the instruction to start warming up by himself.

Nobody had a better angle on Costa's body than Pitillas, who had nursed him back from his most serious injury and watched him transform into an unstoppable force in La Liga. He knew about hamstring injuries. He knew how, without the proper rest, they sat like a time bomb, ready to explode again. He knew that Costa would never admit defeat until that happened.

Pitillas is right on the money. One by one the players realise that Costa is not right. Eight minutes in, Sergio Ramos has worked it out. In possession as the last defender, with Costa 10 yards away, he knows his old rival cannot shut him down and Ramos merely jogs round him with the ball at his feet. Soon after that, Adrián replaces Costa.

After 35 minutes, Atlético take the lead with another huge Diego Godín header, which drifts over Iker Casillas and in as the goalkeeper tries to recover his position. After that, it's a simple equation: Atlético's famous resilience, fuelled by whatever is left in their legs after this gruelling campaign, versus the clock, and Real Madrid's relentless attacking machine. Simeone's men come up short by two minutes 10 seconds. That is how long is left in added time when Sergio Ramos, the player against whom Costa's La Liga legend has been defined more than any other, moves across the box and jumps into a header that flies past Courtois. Atlético are drained. They had paced themselves for 90 minutes. They fell after 92. Another 30? Out of the question.

Extra time was painful viewing for anyone not willing Real Madrid to *La Decima*, their tenth European Cup title. Gareth Bale headed in from point-blank after Courtois had saved from Ángel Di María. Marcelo walked past dead-legged defenders before rolling a low shot into the corner. Then Cristiano Ronaldo won a penalty and lifted it into the net. Simeone loses it in the closing stages of the match, running onto the pitch to confront Raphael Varane after the defender kicks the ball toward the coach. It all comes down around Atlético.

Costa was at the centre of the post-mortem. Had he and Atlético been more realistic about his condition, Simeone would have had another vital substitution to make, a fresh player with which to try to kill the clock.

Costa, his coach and key members of the staff had talked throughout the build-up to the final. They had the information. They took a risk, knowing the possible consequences. And they got it wrong.

Simeone: "It wasn't Diego's fault, because he wanted to play and give his best. Possibly, if I had been in his place as a player, I would have done the exact same, and possibly another coach in my place would have done the same too. Why? Because it's a one off game in which a player of Diego Costa's quality had to be given the chance to say 'I've lost the battle, but I lost it

45 minutes in'. Truthfully, we didn't expect to lose him in the seventh minute. Like it or not, in the scheme of the game, it sadly took away one of our substitutes that could have been decisive."

With an extra substitute, perhaps the outcome would have been different. With a fully fit Diego Costa? From all the evidence of the previous 60 matches in 2013-14, almost certainly so.

Costa ended the season with a league winner's medal, a battered body, one eye on the World Cup and the other on a move to England.

"It was," said Costa, "the most amazing season of my life."

AN INTERNATIONAL INCIDENT

'Having collected his army and amassed his forces,
the general must blend and harmonise the different
elements thereof before pitching his camp'

Sun Tzu, *The Art of War*

BACK IN HIS breakthrough season of 2012-13, the Brazilian Football Confederation (CBF) were watching Diego Costa closely. He was called up by the Brazil coach Luiz Felipe Scolari on March 5, 2013, to be part of the squad for their friendlies against Italy and Russia, part of a global tour. He pulled on the *verdeamarelha* jersey for the first time on March 21 for the Italy game in Geneva. Wearing No.17, Costa came on for Fred in the 69th minute but failed to score as the match finished 2-2. Four days later, this time sporting the No.19, he took over from Kaká against the Russians at Stamford Bridge. Fred scored late on to salvage a 1-1 draw.

At the time the rumour was that Costa was not a natural fit within this squad. In his adopted homeland, the prospect of Spanish nationality – primarily a benefit for Atlético in their management of non-EU players – was beginning to be seen as a potential coup for the national team.

"The minute we realised that Atlético were helping him get Spanish nationality, we started to watch him," explains the Spanish team coach, Vicente del Bosque. "It didn't happen overnight. We had to find out how interested the player would be in the idea." As it turned out, Costa was very interested indeed.

"He learned so much here. He basically grew up professionally in this country and I think he decided to play for Spain because he felt the country had taken him to its heart. He was grateful for all the opportunities he'd had here," reflects Paulo Assunção, another Brazilian to play out his career in La Liga.

"I would have done the same thing in his shoes. You're going to be happy in the place people treat you well. Funnily enough, the pair of us watched Iniesta score in the final of the South African World Cup at my place. But back then I didn't imagine for a minute that he would end up playing in the national team alongside Iniesta."

Former team-mates and staffers remember Costa being aware of the opportunities and support he had received in Spain. To these colleagues, his drift toward *La Roja* was not a surprise. "We have a couple of sayings in Spain: 'It's not where you're born but where you flourish' and 'Gratitude is the sign of noble souls',"says Cirilo Gutiérrez, a former kitman for Atlético. "He felt that he owed Spain a lot."

As Costa was weighing up his options, he had on one hand the courtship of Del Bosque, who had watched the raw potential of Costa's early years emerge under his nose, in Madrid, during season 2013-14. On the other was Scolari, coach of Brazil for their home World Cup the following summer, who made it clear that the debate did not concern a player who he regarded as a pivotal member of his team. Their star would be Neymar, and around him he had Hulk and Fred. The feeling of being important, of being wanted, had been vital to Costa's development during his loans and he had fought to achieve that status at Atlético. Del Bosque seemed to understand that. Scolari did not. There were rumours that he viewed Costa as a back-up plan, and that his pursuit, such as it was, of the striker was aimed at ending Spain's chances of claiming the player.

A big part of the problem was Costa's rare career curve. He had left for Europe without ever playing pro football in Brazil. People there simply did not have the same connection that they felt for the other players in the team.

Marcos Senna understood. He left Brazil early in his career and ended up representing Spain, with whom he won Euro 2008. "It's true," he says. "It's part of the culture there. If a player leaves Brazil before he's really made it big, it's very unlikely he'll ever play for the national side. If you've not become a hero in the fans' eyes before you leave, forget it."

By the time of the 2013 Confederations Cup, Scolari had decided to stick with his core of players – including Fred, the striker who had shared the top of the goalscorers' chart at that tournament with Fernando Torres and scored twice in the final on June 30, as Brazil defeated Spain 3-0. When Fred tired toward the end of that game, he was replaced by Jô.

In October 2013, with Fred injured and Costa tearing up La Liga, Scolari was pranked by El Groupe Risa, a radio comedy troupe who called up the coach, pretending to be Enrique Cerezo, the president of Atlético. Scolari, in a call broadcast on the show *El Partido de las 12*, now said that "if the World Cup was today, I would bring Diego to Brazil. The first choice is Fred, who is injured. Diego is second".

By November, Costa had decided to change allegiances on the pitch.

"This is not a rejection of Brazil as my homeland. That's where I was born and where I want to live when I retire," he insisted. "It's just that in Spain people really value what I do. Until now I have always adhered to a certain philosophy and I believe that I have chosen the place where I am loved and wanted. In Spain people respect what I do day in, day out, my career has flourished here and I have always felt welcomed. It has been a very difficult decision but I can honestly say that Spain has given me everything."

Even the player's father had advised his son to opt for *La Roja* and Costa himself was so sure of his decision that in early November he gave both Julio César Avelleda, secretary general of the CBF and FIFA, formal notice that he would like to play for Spain. He asked the Brazilian authorities to remove his name from the squad lists for the upcoming friendlies against Honduras and Chile.

The response from Brazil was frosty. "Any player who says he does not wish to wear the Brazil jersey and rejects the chance to compete in the World Cup in his own country, should expect to be rejected automatically. Diego Costa is turning his back on the dreams of millions of people," snarled Scolari.

Feelings continued to run high and Carlos Eugenio Lopes, the director of the CBF's legal department, told *O Globo* newspaper that CBF president José María Marín (ironically of Spanish parentage himself) had authorised a petition which requested that the Brazilian Ministry of Justice rescind all of the player's rights as a citizen. Lopes himself suggested that Costa had come under pressure from the Spanish federation and that the player's decision was driven by purely economic reasons. In the end none of the official threats came to anything, but anger about Costa's decision continued to be voiced in the country at large. One car dealer in the state of Ceará expressed their outrage through an advertising slogan: 'Unlike Diego Costa, this car is something Brazilians can be proud of.'

Eventually even Pelé himself felt duty bound to enter the fray and, whilst expressing his regret that Costa would not be in the national team, insisted:

"Diego has shown a lot of courage and we should all respect his decision." Despite having officially declared his decision in the presence of a lawyer, bureaucratic complications prevented Costa from joining the Spain squad immediately. A press release issued by the Spanish federation explained that Costa was "in the process of complying with certain additional conditions set down by FIFA". It now looked like he would make his debut for Spain on their tour of Africa.

No sooner had he received official confirmation that he would be included in the squad than Costa's luck took a turn for the worse. As he warmed up for a match against Villarreal in the Madrigal, he felt a twinge in his thigh. The problem was then exacerbated by his countryman Gabriel Paulista, whose robust defending resulted in Costa being substituted. Ice was immediately applied to the player's thigh but an MRI scan the following day confirmed the bad news: he had an injury (grade 1-2) in his adductor muscle. Along with chief medic Dr José María Villalón, the player travelled to the Spanish federation's headquarters in Las Rozas to consult doctors Óscar Luis Celada and Juan Cota, who told him that he would be out of action for 10 days and would therefore miss the friendlies against Equatorial Guinea and South Africa. The Juventus player Fernando Llorente took Costa's place and the Brazilian resigned himself to the delay.

"These things happen in football. The lad's suffering

but it's important that he takes a break," commented Del Bosque.

From the start, Costa had developed a strong relationship with the national coach. Prior to November, the two men had met over lunch to chat about the future.

"There are always people who object to new signings," says Del Bosque. "I wasn't interested in the gossip and preferred to meet the player and make up my own mind. We had lunch together and I found [Costa] charming and very down to earth. I was very impressed. In person he is completely different from that aggressive player we all see on the pitch. We had a great chat and he was easy company. The fact that he was there at all says a lot about him. His is certainly a unique situation but I have never asked him why he didn't choose Brazil. He has complied with all the requirements to qualify for Spanish citizenship and that's enough for me."

By February 28, 2014, things were looking brighter when Del Bosque announced that Costa would be part of the 21-man squad for the match against Italy on March 5. The decision was celebrated with a fireworks display over Lagarto, in his home country. Cars blared their horns. People wore Spain shirts.

"People are talking about it on every street corner and in ever bar in town," Mayor Lila Fraga told the EFE news agency. "We understand what he's done. If Brazil and Spain end up playing we'll all be supporting Brazil, but we'll want a 2-1 scoreline, with a goal from Diego Costa".

His old buddy Prefeitinho now worked for a radio station back home, which carried out a survey of listeners in Lagarto. Seventy percent said they were behind Costa. "People in Lagarto are supporting two national teams: Brazil and Diego," said Prefeitinho. "A town councillor has even suggested that we erect a monument to him!"

Costa joined his new team-mates on March 3. He arrived early at Las Rozas wearing a t-shirt and cotton jacket to find his club team-mates, Juanfran and Koke, waiting for him. After the official welcome, the striker quickly changed and prepared himself for his first training session with Spain. Meanwhile, Simeone was telling Radio Marca: "He is the best possible injection of talent the Spain team could get. He is unique."

During that first training session Costa stayed close to his Atlético team-mates, who were happy to give him advice and support. He also took time to chat to Álvaro Negredo as the squad ran out onto the pitch and to catch up with his La Liga sparring partner Sergio Ramos.

Ramos welcomed Costa's arrival in the squad, saying: "He's earned the right to be here and is a great choice. Now that he's my team-mate, we'll treat each other differently. We hope to see the very best of him when he plays for Spain."

Del Bosque talked to Costa throughout the session and Costa smiled conspiratorially at the coach whilst he did his stretches. "I really liked the míster the minute I met him," was the player's verdict. "I want to prove myself here after all that has been said and done over the last few months. I reckon the Spain shirt suits me pretty well."

Huge screens had been mounted in bars all over Lagarto to show the Italy game. Costa was about to become the fifth Brazilian (or the sixth if you count Thiago Alcántara, who was actually born in Italy) to play for Spain.

Costa said: "I never dreamt I'd end up playing for Spain so I was blown away when the federation contacted me," said Costa. "I had already played for Brazil and that was a dream come true, but I really feel needed and appreciated in Spain. I don't want people to make it easy for me. I have to earn my place."

Nobody in the Spain camp had promised Costa anything, but Del Bosque showed the kind of faith in Costa that had been lacking in the country of his birth.

"I had no worries about him causing trouble in the dressing room," says Del Bosque. "I knew nothing would happen. He's a good lad. We don't need him to change. In fact, we like him exactly the way he is."

"I have no intention of upsetting anyone or winding up the other players," promised the striker.

Word got out early afternoon that Costa would start

against Italy. The superstitious striker was the only player to cross himself as he hopped onto the pitch of the Vicente Calderón, right foot first. An imposing figure standing in between the much shorter Jordi Alba and César Azpilicueta, Costa stared off into the distance as if in deep thought. As the national anthem finished the player jumped a couple of times and then fell onto his knees for a quick prayer. He had time for a word with Thiago and Pedro before the whistle sounded for the start of the game.

Costa was on the ball almost immediately. The first thing he did, after an Iniesta pass sent him into open space, was to barge into Gabriel Paletta, who was marking him, and the ref blew for a foul. From that point on it was as if he remembered where he was and reined himself in. Timid. Tempted to show his claws, but too anxious to do so. His game looked better when he was played into space than when he was asked to participate in complex build-up play. He didn't shoot on goal until the 81st minute, but he worked ceaselessly and Paletta, also making his debut that day for an adopted national team, patrolled him well. After the match, Costa would head straight for the Italo-Argentine to shake his hand.

Spain scraped a win with a goal from Pedro. "The first game is never easy. I'm happy with my performance but I know I can do so much better," he said.

"It's very hard when you know all the cameras are on

you, but he's happy here and wants to continue playing for Spain," said Iker Casillas, Costa's new captain.

Adapting to a different style of football was going to be a challenge to Costa, whose new role would be to provide solutions when opponents opted to 'park the bus' and play defensively against Spain.

"He's different from the strikers we already have and he will complement them wonderfully," explained Del Bosque. "He's a natural phenomenon, full of drive, who doesn't stop working off the ball. This was his debut and it was natural for him to want to prioritise the team and to make less use of his individual skill."

That remit – to break down the defences that Spain had faced at successive tournaments – put Costa in pole position for the striker's job at the World Cup – if he stayed fit.

Fran Mérida was a team-mate at Atlético who had moved to Brazil to play with Atlético Paranaense. "I love winding people up about it here," he said at the time. "I tell them that they have no idea what this guy's like and that he'll score the winner in the final."

"If he does score the winner, he'd be best not to venture out onto the streets afterwards because there will be some pretty angry people about," added Marcos Senna.

"People are going to whistle him and will want to provoke him. But in his shoes I'd go with a clear conscience," reflected Donato, the Brazilian who played for Atlético and then Spain at Euro 96.

"The more difficult something is, the more satisfying it is," concluded Costa.

By the time the World Cup came into focus, the difficulty for Costa had been amplified by the injuries that had blighted the end to the season in Spain.

Twenty days separated the Champions League final which Costa had been forced to abort and Spain's opening game in the World Cup, a rematch of the 2010 final against Holland. Once again an equation was being assessed, with the strength of Costa's hamstring on one side and the need to have him in the team on the other. This time the man making the decision was not Diego Simeone, but Vicente del Bosque.

They landed in Curitiba, Brazil, in the early hours of the morning of June 9, in heavy rain and with a hard-faced and heavily-armed military escort, the response to public protests against the economic rationale of Brazil's hosting of the World Cup.

By this point, it appeared that Del Bosque had made a decision: if the striker was fit to play, Costa would be his starter. This despite David Villa – Spain's all-time leading goalscorer, who had announced his intention to retire from international football after the World Cup – scoring twice after coming off the bench in the final warm-up match, against El Salvador in Washington, D.C. Costa played 74 minutes in that game, his biggest test since the Champions League final. He had made it through, but it was Villa and not he who had made the biggest impact. The two Atlético strikers had been in direct competition for the first goal, but as Costa leaned back, poised to volley in a Sergio Ramos knockdown, Villa nipped in front to head it off his boot. The veteran was just that little bit sharper.

In training at their Curitiba base, Costa was not quite up to speed. His finishing was not sharp and some of the highly technical passing and small-sided drills seemed to pass him by. Del Bosque's three-time champion squad was proving a difficult group to break in to.

As always, however, Costa had no problems in terms of personality. By now he and Ramos had formed the most unlikely of friendships, considering their wars on the pitch for both Madrid clubs. He goofed around with Sergio Busquets, the stern Barcelona midfielder. When they moved to their beach-side hotel in Salvador, for the Holland game, it was Costa who could be seen taking air, alone, while he waited outside to give tickets to friends and family. He appeared happy, confident, at ease. Not in the least like a man with one nation against him, and the expectations of another on his shoulders.

Even during training, Costa had been assaulted with chants of 'Traitor!' from the galleries. From the moment he emerged onto the pitch in Salvador ahead of the Holland game, he was bombarded.

Traitor! Traitor! Traitor!
*Hey, Diego! Go f*** yourself!*

Diego, you c***!
Booooooooooo!

Costa's first big play of the World Cup did not enhance his standing among Brazilians outside of Lagarto. He took a Xavi pass into the box and drew a foul from Stefan De Vrij, ensuring that a sliding challenge from the defender took him down. Replays later showed that Costa has stood on the defender's leg. Xabi Alonso converted to give Spain the edge. From a sublime Andrés Iniesta pass, David Silva missed a golden opportunity to make it 2-0 when his tame chipped effort was easily held by Dutch goalkeeper Jasper Cillessen. After that, Spain's World Cup began to disintegrate.

Robin Van Persie's iconic strike made it 1-1 at half-time – the Manchester United player escaping the attentions of Sergio Ramos to loop an incredible 15-yard header over Casillas.

The second half became a surrender. Costa was replaced by Fernando Torres after Arjen Robben's goal made it 2-1. De Vrij extinguished hopes of a comeback when he forced home Wesley Sneijder's free-kick – with the referee ignoring claims by Casillas that he had been impeded by Van Persie – and the chances began to pile up.

There was no question as to Casillas' liability for the fourth goal, the Spanish No.1 mis-controlling a back pass and being dispossessed by Van Persie who scored. Robben's incredible solo goal for Holland's fifth, in which he raced from his own half, outpaced Ramos and smashed it past two defenders on the line, shovelled further salt in the wounds. It was a stunning display of ineptitude, particularly in defence, by the reigning world champions. Amid the outcry, Del Bosque attempted to offer a more measured perspective.

"They were better in the second half after a first half when we played well. They looked to knock the ball over the top against our defence and found a lot of space. We kept on fighting but they were physically stronger as the game went on and that made a difference."

There was so much to talk about after one of the most dramatic matches in World Cup history, but still there was room to pick over a strangely impotent performance from Costa, and the vitriolic treatment he received from the fans.

"Not even Mazzola, who played for Brazil in 1958 and for Italy in 1962, got such an angry reaction," said four-time World Cup champion Mario Zagallo. "Diego was probably ready for this, but you have to admit it was a huge blow for his morale. To make it even worse, he didn't play well at all. To be a Brazilian playing for someone else in the Brazil World Cup wasn't very wise."

Despite most of the big names from the Spain camp making themselves unable for interview, Costa faced reporters after a devastating result.

"Just like I had the right to choose [to play for Spain], they [the supporters] also have the right to do what they want," he said. "They have the option to boo or not. I was aware that it could happen. I am calm and I am proud to play for Spain and in no moment have I doubted my choice."

Spain and Del Bosque now faced enormous decisions. Their match against Chile, in Rio, would carry the threat of elimination. It was a situation they had encountered four years previously, in South Africa, when they had overcome an opening defeat to become champions of the world. That time, however, they had lost by a single goal to Switzerland, who had defended heroically in a match dominated by Del Bosque's team. This time they had been pulverised by Holland, and several key players had not performed – Costa among them.

The Spanish media predicted change. David Villa, overlooked not only in favour of Costa but also left on the bench when Torres came on in Salvador, looked like the sharpest striker in training. Costa looked like he was carrying the burden of a gruelling season and the injuries that had peppered its closing stages. Casillas' place was considered to be up for grabs after a series of errors. There was criticism of the central defensive pairing of Pique and Ramos, and of Xavi.

Only Pique and Xavi dropped out of the starting line-up – replaced by Javi Martínez and Pedro respectively.

Once again Costa appeared blunt at the top of Spain's team. Once again Spain fell short collectively, conceding two first-half goals to Chile – with strikes from Eduardo Vargas and Charles Aránguiz – and never looked like they would be capable of a comeback. Costa lasted 64 minutes – two more than in Salvador. His only positive contribution had been an aerial overhead kick that had presented Busquets with a golden chance from close range, which the midfielder had missed.

Again, Costa was replaced by Torres, not Villa. Again, he had been subjected to the most vicious of treatment by the Brazilian crowd.

His World Cup was over, as was the case for many of Del Bosque's first picks. Costa had clocked 126 minutes. He had touched the ball 50 times and not one of his five attempts on goal had found the target. In the UK, the Daily Mail newspaper ran a piece asking whether Chelsea were about to sign another misfiring forward, comparing his performances at the World Cup to the disappointing domestic form of the London club's roster of forwards: Torres, Samuel Eto'o and Demba Ba.

During training, Cesc Fàbregas had his starter's bib taken from him by Del Bosque, apparently judged by his coach to be suffering from the kind of malaise Alonso had described.

In their final group match – a dead rubber against Australia – Del Bosque made seven changes, including starting Villa and Torres. Both scored in a 3-0 win.

Costa remained on the bench. His return to Brazil had turned into a nightmare.

The verdicts on Spain's failures were damning, with Xabi Alonso the most vociferous of critics. "We have been unable to maintain the hunger and perhaps our quota of success has come to an end. We made many mistakes.

"All cycles come to an end with defeat. And this one has hurt. Some things are going to have to change: we did not arrive mentally prepared. Physically, we were also at the limit and we were unable to control the situations. Our pride is hurt."

The post-mortem lasted beyond the end of the tournament, and criticism was by no means reserved for Costa alone. However, it was a point to which Del Bosque was forced to return. In an interview in September 2014, he reviewed the decision-making process and came up with a different assessment of Costa's fitness to the one made by he and his staff in the build-up to the tournament.

"I have gone all the way back to the beginning, I've looked at the squad and I don't think I strayed far from what the majority of people would have done," said Del Bosque.

"The starting line-up wasn't much different to one chosen by the readers of a newspaper the day before [the first match], it was the same. So we didn't do anything particularly strange.

"We didn't operate well as a group. The most striking thing is that we trained well and the attitude of the players was magnificent, even in the four days leading up to the Australia match. The players still had a great attitude, which wasn't easy. We trained well and they were very involved. There weren't any problems.

"If you want to get into details, you could think that Diego Costa wasn't 100%, but I don't want to place the focus on anything in particular – that wouldn't be fair. I don't want to make excuses either but I think we didn't connect with him. We didn't get accustomed to him as we should have done. But he clearly didn't arrive fully fit. Diego is a great kid and fitted in perfectly.

"Some of the criticism has been hurtful. A journalist described it as wretched. In sport, there are no defeats with a wretched attitude. It was a disaster, we played badly, but we were not wretched.

"We have a wonderful group of players. Occasionally someone would have a long face but that's inevitable, everyone wants to play."

A familiar narrative had formed. A coach who desperately wanted to select the Diego Costa he had seen terrorising La Liga, had looked at the information in front of him and seen only what he wanted to see. Just as Diego Simeone came to regret selecting Costa for the Champions League final, so Del Bosque looked back on the World Cup and saw things differently in retrospect. In both cases, Costa's iron-clad conviction had worked against himself and his team, convincing everyone around him that he was capable of operating at his fearsome best.

The damage sustained during a seismic season with Atlético would claim yet more from Costa, but his time in Spain's capital was over. During the World Cup, Costa-to-Chelsea had become the most open of secrets. Soon, the 26-year-old would be on his way to London. There, in less than a single season, his entire story would be reproduced in microcosm: the goals, the controversies and the hamstring that would not heal.

11

CHELSEA: GOING TO WAR

'Let your plans be dark and impenetrable as night,
and when you move, fall like a thunderbolt'

Sun Tzu, *The Art of War*

THE PLAYERS ARRIVING at Stamford Bridge during the summer of 2014 would be crucial to the success or failure of Jose Mourinho's second spell in charge of Chelsea. The previous season had been one of assessment. Mourinho identified three key areas he would focus his resources on: left-back, central midfield and striker. And of those three, there was one clear priority. The deal for Diego Costa had been in the works for a full year and now, finally, he was a Chelsea player.

"First was the striker," said Mourinho in July 2014, once his business had been concluded and his squad was in preparation for the new season. "During the whole [of last] season, the first away goal one of my strikers scored was at Southampton, on New Year's Day. Fernando [Torres] got three, [Demba] Ba a couple, [Samuel] Eto'o didn't score a single goal away from home.

"I've known Diego since he came to Portugal from Brazil at the age of 17. He is a guy whose life was not easy, nobody gave him anything for free and he always had to fight a lot. He is afraid of nothing, ready for everything.

"What jumps out immediately when you see him is his physical and psychological profile: a big, strong guy, using his body, attacking spaces, holding up the ball and pressing people. But he's much more than that. His movement is incredible, the intelligence is amazing, the choices he makes in terms of movement are fantastic. He is ready. He doesn't need a mentor. He is a made player – an end product, a complete striker." English football was about to discover that Mourinho's assessment was pretty much spot on.

Costa's debut was on August 18, at Burnley, and Chelsea went behind early. But Costa scored soon after, blasting the ball through a crowd after a Branislav Ivanović cross had deflected onto the post and out to the striker. By half-time Chelsea were 3-1 up and the game was over.

On the 23rd, Leicester came to Stamford Bridge and Costa had two in two. He broke the resistance of the newly-promoted club off another Ivanović cross, controlling on his chest and then stabbing the ball past Kasper Schmeichel.

"It looks like he's tailor-made for the Premier League," said Alan Shearer, the former England captain and the division's record goalscorer. In the coming weeks, as Costa became the focus of English football, he would find no stronger champion than Shearer, who appeared enthralled by the arrival of a striker with a game so close to his own: powerful, direct and ruthless.

Two days before Chelsea's next match, reports out of their Cobham training ground claimed that Costa had limped out of training with a hamstring problem. It was the first red flag on the injury that would limit his performance in the coming season, but this time it was soon forgotten. Costa reappeared for a 6-3 win at Everton, and scored twice.

Costa scored before Everton touched the ball, and for the first – but not the last – time it was from a Cesc Fàbregas assist. The pass came the instant the striker made his move beyond the Everton defence and, confronted by Tim Howard, Costa tucked a low finish between the sprawling legs of the American goalkeeper.

It was the perfect introduction to Diego Costa. Two clinical finishes – the second from a breakaway in the final minute – a yellow card and a series of confrontations. Notably, Costa was cautioned for roughing up Seamus Coleman, the Everton defender, at a throw-in. Then, when Coleman scored an own goal, Costa mocked him, and Howard flew out of his goal to confront the striker, earning a yellow card of his own.

"He gave the complete centre-forward display," said Phil Neville, another former England international.

Two weeks later, Chelsea 4 Swansea 2 and another three goals for Costa – the only show in town. Once again, Costa had reportedly been a doubt to play. Once again, you never would have guessed it.

Chelsea were behind and playing poorly when Costa outmuscled everyone in the box to head in from a corner. His second was a one-touch finish from a Fàbregas cut-back. Finally he read a rolled pass from Ramires, moving off the shoulder of the last defender for another instant, close-range finish.

Costa had seven goals from his first four games – the best start by any striker in the Premier League. Jose Mourinho was growing accustomed to being asked about him in the post-match press conferences. "If the team plays well, he has to score goals," said the manager. "Seven goals in four Premier League matches is maybe a bit too much – we cannot expect him to have, say, 14 after eight games – but the way he's playing … if he keeps scoring as he is, that will give us a chance to stay at the top.

"He hasn't surprised me. Maybe seven in four has surprised me – that's not normal – but he's comfortable in the team. We were building the side in a way where we were waiting for a certain type of striker. I think everyone knows now why Chelsea did well to wait for Diego rather than buying someone else in the midwinter last season."

Shearer again led a growing army of admirers in the media. "Everything impressed me about Diego Costa today," he said. "He is looking the real deal. When it is not going as it should be for Chelsea, they have a goalscorer who can get them out of it.

"When you consider it took Fernando Torres 43 games to get seven goals, Costa definitely makes a difference. He is always available. He always wants the ball to feet and if you want to push him around and bully him it is alright because he will do the same to you.

"As well as goals, he can assist also. He can do pretty much everything. He has made a great start. He will get a bagful of goals this season if he stays fit, because that team will create chances for him."

Chelsea began their Champions League campaign on September 17, at home to Schalke, and were held to a 1-1 draw. In what would prove something of a landmark decision, Mourinho benched Costa for all bar the final 15 minutes, despite his team's struggles. Afterwards, the manager revealed the fragility of his star striker's hamstring.

"Diego Costa is not in a condition to play three matches in a week," said the coach. "He has problems at this moment. When he plays one game he needs a week to recover to be in condition to play in the next game. We play now in midweek – he can't do it. If he starts [in this game] maybe I have to change him after 25 minutes." Mourinho had established a principle for getting Costa through the season. Could he stick to it?

When the next game is against the champions of England, that decision becomes crystal clear. Next up for Chelsea was Manchester City, Costa's first match for his new club against another of the established forces of the Premier League. The storylines around Costa included now his history with Sergio Agüero, whom he had understudied at Atlético, and Martin Demichelis, one of many defenders with a history of entanglements with Costa. Costa was asked about both in the build-up to Chelsea's trip to Manchester.

"I knew Sergio at Atlético, he was God and I loved watching him. He is, for me, the best I saw play. I learnt a lot playing alongside him," said the striker.

And on the attention from defenders: "There is a perception people have of my character. Some will look for any way to try to take advantage. It's happening here. It happened in Spain. Wherever I play it will always be like that," he said. "If people provoke me, I'll put goals past them. The reality is, for the moment, I haven't had any really physical battles. Things have been going well. I'm enjoying it."

At the Etihad, Costa's streak came to an end, but Chelsea earned a point from a gruelling encounter. The striker had a bruising contest with Vincent Kompany, the City centre-back, struck a post and was also involved in the confrontation that led to a red card for Pablo Zabaletta, the City full-back.

Chelsea lost out on all three points when their record goalscorer, Frank Lampard, equalised for City late on, but there now began a debate around whether

Mourinho's men could complete the league season unbeaten. Already, it seemed, they had assumed the role of short-priced favourites for the championship.

In his next league game, Costa was back on target, heading goal No.8 of the season in a 3-0 win over Aston Villa. The striker also created a goal for Willian with a skilful dribble and shot that produced a rebound which his fellow Brazilian converted. Costa left the field to a standing ovation.

After a narrow win over Sporting in Lisbon in the Champions League, Chelsea faced another of the Premier League big guns – Arsenal. A 2-0 win for Mourinho's men produced two talking points. Firstly, could Chelsea repeat the achievement of Arsenal's famous Invincibles of 2003-04. Secondly, who could stop the Fàbregas-Costa axis?

After Eden Hazard had created and scored a penalty, it was the two new signings who sealed the victory for Chelsea. From deep within his own half, Fàbregas launched a quarter-back pass over the top of the Arsenal defence and into the path of Costa, who controlled on his chest and deftly touched the ball over the advancing Wojciech Szczesny.

Around this time, Mourinho was asked about his recruitment of Fàbregas. If the foundations for the Costa deal were laid the previous summer, the move for his supplier in chief was much more decisive. Once it became clear that Fàbregas would leave Barcelona for a second time, Arsenal had an option to buy the player back, but declined. Manchester United wanted the Spaniard, but, it appeared, only after their first target, Thiago, chose Bayern Munich.

"I was objective with him," said Mourinho. "I gave him the different possibilities – 'with me you will play here, not there. This is the way we want to play, this is the way we are going to develop the team. No way with me are you going to play fake No.9, outside-left, outside-right. What I need is this, this and this.' Everything was so clean.

"We spoke about football. We spoke about the Chelsea project. We spoke about the way I want him to play, the way I want to transform my team."

In an enlightening interview with football analyst Gary Neville in October, Mourinho further expanded on the difference both Costa and Fàbregas had made.

"So [last season] my team was unstable. This season we improve footballistically, with Diego and Fàbregas, no doubt. When we analyse in tactical and technical terms, they represent the kind of player we need, the kind of second midfield player, the quality of striker. We were lucky to have in the market available for us exactly the style of player we need. But what people maybe don't realise is that the maturity of our team, the personality of our team, changed a lot."

The telepathy which quickly developed between Fàbregas and Costa overlooked the fact that, while

Costa was an archetypal Mourinho striker – power, pace and finishing – Fàbregas did not quite fit the mould of the qualities he usually looks for in his midfielders. The former Chelsea and Scotland winger Pat Nevin, who writes a column for the club's website and analyses games on Radio Five Live, initially raised an eyebrow at the acquisition of the former Arsenal midfielder. "Fàbregas surprised me slightly," he admitted. "He's not the quickest and Jose likes quick players. He's also playing deeper than I expected.

"Throughout my career I had two or three players who I had a perfect understanding with. It would be a case of 'you know what I can do' and the ball would arrive at my feet. Costa and Fàbregas have that kind of understanding.

"I would compare it to a quarterback playing with a wide receiver. The wide receiver knows the plays and when he turns round the ball is there. It is exactly the same with Costa and Fàbregas, though the plays aren't planned – it is just pure football intelligence. I think a similar relationship exists between Hazard and Diego, and also Hazard and Oscar."

Costa had nine goals from seven Premier League appearances when he rejoined the Spain squad for a double header in Slovakia and Luxembourg, both qualifiers for Euro 2016.

Spain lost 2-1 in Zilina in front of a crowd of less than 10,000. The result looked like a World Cup hangover, right down to the big error by Iker Casillas, who was confused by a free-kick by Juraj Kucka which moved only a little in the air. Costa was no longer the disconnected, half-fit striker he had been in Brazil, however. Matus Kozacik, the Slovakian goalkeeper, twice came up with the goods to deny Costa his first Spain goal – first from a strong header and then after the striker had beaten two defenders to give himself a sight of goal. Still, after Paco Alcacer's equaliser, Spain gave up a late goal on a break and once again were heavily criticised.

Against Luxembourg there was no such drama. Costa, however, did not emerge unscathed. After David Silva opened the scoring, Alcacer's third goal in three internationals underlined the fact that Costa was still looking for his first in seven. That came in the second half, and after a series of missed opportunities. Costa controlled a wayward shot from Sergio Busquets and, on the six-yard line, turned and shot into an empty net. Relief replaced joy in his celebration. On the bench, Casillas provided proof that Del Bosque's patience with even his most trusted players was not without end.

There would be a cost. He would not play again in October, missing three matches after returning from international duty with damage to the hamstring injury that appeared resistant to everything Chelsea and Costa did to mend it. It was also reported that Costa had spent time in hospital suffering symptoms similar to a severe stomach bug, returning to Chelsea in a state that did not please the club.

Mourinho, it was reported, had asked Del Bosque to use his man sparingly, but Costa had played all but the final eight minutes of the two internationals across four days. The Chelsea manager had predicted the consequences of such intense action a month previously, when he benched Costa in the Champions League. Now, due to events over which he had no control, he had been proven correct.

Costa came back on November 1, playing 78 minutes of a 2-1 win against QPR. Four days later he was a half-time substitute in the Champions League. Mourinho perhaps felt pressure to break his own rule as his side struggled to another 1-1 draw, this time in Maribor. Then three days later he asked Costa to lead the line in another huge Premier League match, against Liverpool.

He was rewarded with a winning goal, sealing a come-from-behind 2-1 victory at Anfield. Costa's header had led to Gary Cahill's equaliser and when César Azpilicueta wormed his way into a crossing position down the left, the striker peeled off at the back post to hammer a low finish through a crowd.

It was an important moment, a franking of Chelsea's title ambitions, and their manager was quick to praise the victory which moved them 15 points clear of their Anfield hosts.

Mourinho said: "In the second half, against Liverpool, at Anfield, every team accepts a point as a good result. My team didn't accept that, so the way they performed in the second half was an expression of that ambition and self-belief they have at the moment. Sometimes you get points you don't deserve but this is a case where the best team won. I do not believe we will go through the season unbeaten but, if we do lose a game, it will not have an impact."

Costa was withdrawn late on at Anfield, and then missed Spain's Euro 2016 qualifier against Belarus – a 3-0 win – and a friendly defeat by Germany. The hamstring injury, it seemed, was now providing the ammunition in a tit-for-tat between club and country. He was well rested for the next Premier League game, a 2-0 win over West Brom. Costa scored a sublime opener, controlling with his chest and then volleying in his 11th of the season. Then, all before the half-hour mark, Fàbregas scored and Claudio Yacob was red carded for a violent tackle on Costa, who had been targeted by West Brom from the outset.

Fàbregas, the former Arsenal and Barcelona midfielder who had quickly established himself as Chelsea's creative fulcrum, admitted that he had rarely experienced such a high standard of football in his career. "The first half [against West Brom], I don't think I am exaggerating if I say I don't remember playing and enjoying a football match as much as this."

After a 5-0 win over Schalke in the Champions League in which Costa was withdrawn early, consecutive trips to the north-east slowed down Chelsea's rocket-powered start to the season. After a 0-0 draw at Sunderland, the Invincible project died in Newcastle, where the home side won 2-1 with goalkeeper Jak Alnwick making his pro debut, and despite losing Steven Taylor to a red card with 15 minutes left to play.

As Chelsea entered the frenetic Christmas period – a new experience for Costa – Mourinho was using the striker with less caution. He played five times in 13 days between December 22 and January 4, although by the last of these, a 3-0 home win over Watford, he was a half-time substitute. He scored twice in this sequence, wrapping up a 2-0 win against West Ham and again in Chelsea's second league defeat, in a 5-3 thriller against Tottenham on New Year's Day. That game also featured a double from Harry Kane, Spurs' emerging centre-forward who would become Costa's primary early-season challenger in the race for the Golden Boot. Despite defeat, Chelsea began 2015 exactly level with Manchester City at the top of the table – tied on points, goal difference and goals scored.

Costa then scored three in two league games – one as revenge was gained over Newcastle and two more against his favourite opponents, Swansea. His first in that game, and the goal against Newcastle, were both fine team goals. With Costa, Fàbregas, Oscar and

Hazard forming a formidable offensive unit, Chelsea looked every inch champions elect as they surged in front of City. "It was the perfect game for us, everything went in our direction," said Mourinho. "The team was solid defensively and in attack obviously they took chances and were aggressive in the way they thought about their football. They had ambition, so it was a good performance. But I keep saying, and they have to understand, there is no history without titles. So if we play fantastically well but we don't win cups, then in 20 years' time nobody will remember this team."

If Costa's goalscoring had powered Chelsea's season to date, then the overall fluency of their attacking play owed much to the focal point he offered at the head of their team. It was becoming increasingly obvious that he was more than just a traditional target man. Nevin was struck by the subtlety of his all-round game as it dovetailed with the attacking instincts of Oscar and Hazard, as well as Fàbregas.

"A lot of people look at the goals scored and his rate has been good without being off the scale," said Nevin. "But that's not where his only strengths are. He's more than just a goalscorer. His hold-up play is superb, he has a better understanding of link-up play than most strikers I've seen; technically he is very good on the ball. He has an understanding with Oscar, Fàbregas and Hazard – and his movement is right up there alongside them, which isn't always the case with strikers.

"You often see him zooming beyond defenders in the inside-left area and because of that, gaps open up behind them which allows space for Oscar, Fàbregas and Hazard to play in. His movement works well in Chelsea's 4-2-3-1 formation. If opponents play with two defensive midfielders, then Costa's movement can drag them out of position, too, and create spaces for the others. That's a big deal for players like Oscar and Hazard. It's an unheralded side of Costa's game. I wouldn't be surprised if Hazard is Chelsea's Player of the Year, but he doesn't always pick the ball up on the wing. Instead, he can play in the spaces that Costa's movement creates."

For now, though, the league would take a back seat. Across eight days in January Chelsea faced a two-legged League Cup semi-final against Liverpool, and in between those games an FA Cup fixture against Bradford City, of League One. Things would get increasingly more dramatic.

Costa was kept pretty quiet at Anfield as Chelsea led, but then were lucky to leave with a 1-1 draw. He was not in the squad for what was seen as a routine tie against lower league opponents in the FA Cup, but Chelsea were undone in one of that tournament's signature upsets. Bradford won 4-2 at Stamford Bridge and, although Mourinho had rested some of his A-listers, the gap in stature, earning power and experience between the two teams was colossal. It was the biggest shock in a weekend that went down in FA Cup history for a series of upsets.

The second leg of the League Cup semi-final ended with Chelsea on their way to Wembley and the final, but their star striker on his way to a three-game ban and the first sign that he had not completely subjugated the devil inside. While he had still yet to be red carded, Costa twice appeared to stamp on opponents – Emre Can and Martin Škrtel. He was also involved in a typically Costa-esque confrontation with Steven Gerrard and, before any of it, should have had a penalty when Škrtel brought him down.

After Branislav Ivanović's header at the start of extra-time had won it for Chelsea, video footage of his clash with Can was reviewed and a three-game suspension enforced. Shortly after news of that punishment came in, Costa was sitting down with Rob Draper of the *Daily Mail*. It provided a rare and in-depth analysis by the player of his own style of play, best summed up by Costa himself as "going to the limit".

"As far as what happened on Tuesday, the main thing is when I get home and I can sleep knowing I've not done anything wrong, because I never meant to do that and it was not on purpose," he said.

"And you can clearly see that on the video. But it is a suspension. I have to accept that, I have to take it. Obviously I feel sad because I'm not going to be able to play or to help the team. But I have to accept and respect it.

"I'm not saying I'm an angel – I'm no angel. You can see that. But every time I play I will play the same way because that's the way I am. That's what I need to do in order to support my family. That's my bread and butter; also that's what I need to do for this club, for the fans and for all the people involved in this club.

"On the pitch I will always be like that. That's my character and I will always compete. I'm a different guy off the pitch – as you can see – but on it I will not change. And I want to say this again: you can look at the video and interpret it how you want but I know I can sleep in peace because I know I didn't mean to do it.

"You have to ask how many times have I injured someone? Never. I've never injured another colleague, another player on purpose. Yes I've had loads of incidents – maybe even more in Spain. But that's the way I play. I'm not going to change the way I play because I got banned for a few games now. I'm always loyal, I always go 100 per cent, I always go to the limit but the people who think I am a violent player, it's because they interpret football a different way.

"Back in the old days there used to be way more contact and a lot of things permitted that, these days, everyone is looking at – and I don't think that is good for the game. I have a go at defenders and they have a go at me, we argue and whatever happens on the pitch stays on the pitch.

"After the game I shake hands with the defender. Job done, I go home, he goes home. We're all mates. It's all good. That's how I see football. That's how I play football. I'm not going to change it – football is a contact sport.

"I really, really like it [in England] because it's very competitive, it's very physical. Here, playing as a striker, you get kicked way more than, for example, Spanish football and referees don't call fouls – not only for me but all strikers in the league."

Costa also spoke about a common theme in his story – the contradiction between his on-field persona and the affable, laid-back man who exists outside of the white lines. It was, he said, his own contribution to a unity of spirit that was as vital to a team's success as the combined talents of its players – perhaps even more so.

"I've always been that way, that's the way I am," he says. "I don't do things for people to think I am funny, that's really the way I am. It comes naturally. I've always liked to joke with every club I've been in, with all my team-mates because it's where we work and we spend a lot of time together, more time than even with your family. So I do like to joke around – but I'm not the only one. There's a few jokers in the dressing room. Didier Drogba is a big one and Eden Hazard as well.

"You can have the best players in the world together but if there is no bond, if there's no group, you cannot achieve anything. A great example of that is what happened at Atlético Madrid last season. We had a group which was brilliant. We were all mates for real, on and off the pitch. We solved all our problems within the dressing room. Nothing ever went out into the press. We all fought for each other and for the club, we all defended each other as mates and that's why we achieved what we did. Here, it is very similar. We have a great bond.

"There are great players like Didier Drogba. I don't have to say what he was or what he is. I'm playing now in his place but he would never be moody or anything like that; same with Ramires. We all go in the same direction. And that's the only way in order to succeed."

Mourinho reacted in vintage fashion, shutting down his squad to the media and initiating a narrative around a campaign against his team. He supported Costa's decision to contest the ban, which was doomed from the beginning and apparently based solely on Costa's determination to have his denial of a deliberate stamp placed on the record.

In the immediate aftermath of the Liverpool game, Costa's impact was expertly summed up by Hazard. When asked if Costa's style of play was a motivational force for the team, the Belgian winger was emphatic: "Yes, yes, yes. When you play with this guy, you have to give everything. You can see in every action and for every ball, he gives his life.

"Even if he didn't score against Liverpool, he gave his

life. For us, for the players, when you play with him, it's very good. In training he is a little different but in the game he is very good. He never stops. He had a very good mentality against Liverpool. We need him because he can score every minute, every second. He did very well."

Hazard's reflections were important in underlining the mentality shift Costa had brought to the club, the edge which forced team-mates to give more to the cause. Nevin, an astute observer of the club, reflected on the intensity he had brought to the team. "Some of that intensity was maybe missing last year. Fernando [Torres] worked very, very hard. Now and again his head would go down, but you don't seem to see that with Diego when it is not happening for him. I remember playing against Kevin Keegan when he was 36, and he was working harder than anyone when his team were 4-0 down with 10 minutes to go. I thought 'that's the way to do it'. Costa is a top international player with the perfect attitude. He's also the perfect Jose player."

The ever-insightful Gary Neville – arguably the leading analyst on English football with a sharp appreciation of how to foster a winning mentality – mounted a robust defence of Costa's style in the aftermath of the Liverpool controversy.

He wrote: "The first line of any book I would write on football philosophy is: 'Be horrible to play against.'

Diego Costa is horrible to play against and I applaud him for it... Costa will get himself in trouble, miss matches, upset people. But I don't buy the outrage. I think it made for a compelling football match, the sort of game I would love to watch, week in, week out. Costa's a catalyst player, because he will have an effect on Eden Hazard, then other Chelsea players, then other teams and the whole of English football. The Chelsea youth-team players will look at him and think: 'This guy is on huge money, yet he looks like he's chasing his last meal every time he runs for the ball.'

"I admit, my tolerance, my line, is different from that of people who watch the game without professional involvement. That doesn't make me right. Nor do I condone poor behaviour – or violence. Yet the idea that Costa's behaviour was violent is nonsense. I don't believe it was highly dangerous, or capable of snapping a leg, which would be despicable. The Škrtel clash was nothing; the Can one was a little bit naughty, no more.

"Every coach is desperate for leaders. Costa is a leader, as Hazard's comments tell us. Sport is not a place for flawless people. Tell me how many flawless people there are in society. The characteristics of role models, often, are a willingness to work hard, fight hard, display passion for a cause. Most coaches are scouring the game for people with these characteristics, and Costa is helping to turn Chelsea from a team who fell short last season into potentially one of the great Premier League teams."

Nevin offered a fascinating revelation on Costa's introduction to the Chelsea dressing room: "When he first came, his English wasn't great. He asked Oscar to relay a message to some of the players – JT, Cahill, Ivanović and Matić. He explained via Oscar how he played and what he was going to do and how he would need physical support at times. The reaction [from the four players] was 'GET IN!' That is massively old school.

"He is very old school in the sense of taking hits and giving hits. Even if he is hit himself, you'll sometimes see him giving his opponent a little low-five as if to say: 'OK, I respect you for that.' 20 or 30 years ago people would respect that and say 'he gives as good as he gets'. Chelsea fans really love that."

Chelsea got through the suspension with fine results – a 1-1 draw against Manchester City that was far better news for the challengers than the champions, and narrow wins over Aston Villa and Everton. Costa would return in the Champions League round of 16. The opponents: Paris St Germain. Chelsea had progressed at the expense of the Paris club in the previous season's quarter-finals when they won on away goals after the tie finished 3-3 on aggregate, with Demba Ba's 87th-minute strike at Stamford Bridge sending them into the last four.

This time, the two ties against Laurent Blanc's team would become landmarks in Chelsea's season, and ensure that the many successes of 2014-15 would not be unblemished. It started in Paris, with a 1-1 draw in which the French club had the better chances, Thibaut Courtois responsible for keeping the score level.

Ivanović's first-half header opened the scoring – his fifth goal of the season but first in Europe since his winner against Benfica in the 2013 Europa League final – but the home side were dominant throughout the second half and scored a deserved equaliser through Edinson Cavani. Cavani and Zlatan Ibrahimović both went close to scoring a winner, the latter's header in stoppage-time being brilliantly saved by Courtois.

Before the rematch in London, Costa had a date at Wembley, and his first cup final as a Chelsea player, against Spurs. Chelsea's victory would be typical of their gear change, from flamboyant, dominant early-season front runners to a more clinical win machine, typical of their manager. Both models usually featured a goal from their No.19 and Costa again obliged. Found by Fàbregas – who else? – his shot deflected off Kyle Walker and in. Any question of credit was settled when Costa spoke to reporters after the game: "It was mine, of course. I shot to the sticks. If I don't shoot there is no goal."

Walker, Nabil Bentaleb and Eric Dier all had their bouts with Costa, but the striker emerged unscathed and smiling, parading his first trophy as a Chelsea player around Wembley in the short window of celebration allowed to Mourinho's men before their next step toward the season's larger objectives.

In the Premier League, this meant a critical 1-0 win at West Ham. This was the sixth consecutive game in which Costa had not scored, and he was not the big story after every match, as he had been at the start of the season. The bad news for opponents of Chelsea was the depth in the attack. Costa may not always score, but he would certainly punch a hole or two in the defence for Oscar, Hazard, Willian and Fàbregas to break through. At Upton Park it was Hazard, with a rare header, who made the difference.

However, in the Champions League, Chelsea and Costa could not deliver. Laurent Blanc had focused on Costa in the build-up to the match at Stamford Bridge. "He likes contact, and provokes opposition players," said the PSG coach. "He thrives off that. The most important thing is to not get caught up in the way he plays."

However, this would be a match mired in contact, real and simulated. Chelsea had the upper hand after 33 minutes, when Ibrahimović was sent off for a clumsy tackle on Oscar. The decision was debatable and the referee surrounded by blue shirts as he made up his mind – with Costa running half the length of the pitch to join his team-mates in lobbying the official. The Swedish striker was not impressed.

"When I got the red card all the Chelsea players came around," he said. "It felt like I had a lot of babies around me. I don't know if I have to get angry or start to laugh. For me when I saw the red card I was like 'the guy [referee] doesn't know what he's doing'. I don't know if he [Oscar] was acting afterwards. Doesn't matter. We won the game."

Chelsea led with nine minutes of regulation time to play, and then again with six minutes of extra-time remaining, but PSG responded to win on away goals. Their first equaliser came from the former Chelsea man David Luiz, the Brazilian with whom Costa had been engaged in an epic war.

The two clashed early on, and Luiz rolled theatrically after a contact the defender himself appeared to initiate. He then confronted Costa, wagging a finger in his chest.

Before the break Luiz elbowed Costa as the two men chased the ball, and was lucky to escape a red card that would have changed the outcome of the evening. When Costa was cautioned for a foul on Thiago Silva, the Brazilian who would score the goal that knocked Chelsea out, Luiz charged in again, falling to the floor as if he had been headbutted by Costa. Luiz, too, was shown a yellow card.

Defeat brought with it a lengthy post-mortem, not just for Chelsea but for the Premier League, who had no representation in the quarter finals of either of Europe's club competitions.

Costa was among those to give his opinion, and suggested that the gruelling December-January calendar left something of a hangover, most noticeable against elite opposition who had not been asked to play at such high intensity and frequency.

"Maybe the Christmas exertions have taken their toll. We played three matches in seven days. It's no excuse though. I'm sure next season we'll go further in the Champions League.

"We had enough quality to play a different game [in London] but it was not to be. PSG have a great team and we have to accept it and congratulate them."

Costa denied that the Premier League, often described from within as the best in the world, had been overinflated, and appeared as happy to be a part of it as it was to have him as one of its star attractions.

"It's a tough league with some great teams in it, I don't think it's overrated," he said. "I take a beating constantly, just like in Spain. But I'm not complaining. They go in hard, but also you don't get the free-kicks you do in Spain. Sometimes defenders try to target me and put me off my game, but my self-control is getting better and I just try to do my thing."

Four days after that disappointment, Chelsea played again and Costa scored for the first time since January. His header was not enough for any more than a point against Southampton, but Mourinho's side were now six points clear and had played a game less than Manchester City.

With Chelsea already red-hot favourites for the title, a trip to Hull did not look like a particularly significant fixture, either for the champions in waiting or for Costa, who led the race for the Golden Boot. However, this was the start of a sequence of events that would end the striker's season.

He scored his 20th goal of the season after nine minutes, curling a beautiful shot in to give his team a 2-0 lead. Earlier in the season, they would have scored more and Costa most likely would have been withdrawn before he put any excessive mileage into his hamstrings. Now, though, they conceded twice in quick succession, and Mourinho dared not substitute his ace until, with 15 minutes left, Costa pulled up, and limped off, clutching the back of his thigh. Again.

Loic Remy, the French striker who had assumed the role of Costa's stand-in taken up by Adrián during Atlético's run-in the previous year, scored almost immediately to give Chelsea a win. In the aftermath, Mourinho fielded questions about Courtois – who had made a rare error, misfielding a backpass for Hull's equalier – and Costa.

"We know his hamstring is not a strong one," said the Chelsea manager. "He works hard in the week to compensate for the weakness he has there but the injury can come.

"He tried to play the Champions League final for Atlético Madrid [last season] and was injured again and again and again. He has this fragility."

It was a telling comparison, both reminding those

listening that Costa was perhaps mishandled by his former club at the end of the previous season, and proving again that Mourinho was acutely aware of the risk-reward equation in place each time Costa was selected to play.

A scan on the hamstring was scheduled for the following day and Costa was withdrawn again from Vicente del Bosque's Spain squad to face Ukraine in a Euro 2016 qualifier and Holland in a friendly. There were 13 days until Chelsea's next Premier League fixture, against Stoke City on April 4.

Álvaro Morata, Juventus' 22-year-old striker, staked his claim for the role at the top of the Spain team with his first international goal as Costa sat out the 1-0 win over Ukraine. A sterile performance in a 2-0 defeat by the Dutch suggested Costa would be welcomed back as soon as he was able.

As was the case at Chelsea. Despite the comfortable position the club were in at the top of the table, and with games against Manchester United and Arsenal on the horizon in April, Mourinho was confident that Costa would make the Stoke game.

The day before the match, he said: "Diego trained yesterday and today with the group and he is not injured. I don't know if I start with him or not because after a muscular injury and then just two days with the group, I need to analyse the situation with him and make a decision.

"His injury was the same as before, hamstring, and he dedicated himself to that with no days off for him or the medical department, working morning and afternoon. We did all the tests and scans to confirm the situation two days ago and at the moment the muscle is fine, but football is more than that, you need confidence, you need to believe you are free to express yourself at the maximum intensity and that is our doubt at the moment. Let's see in the next 24 hours.

"All the season he works on prevention to make the muscle stronger and at the same time elastic and flexible, recovering well with no big accumulation of fatigue. Myself and the medical department always believe that an operation is the last resort for every injury, so we try always to train and recover to compensate the little problems. I don't believe we will ever go to the surgery option [in this case]."

Costa started the game on the bench, and may have remained there had something remarkable not happened. With Chelsea winning 1-0 through Hazard's penalty, and the clock ticking down toward half-time, Charlie Adam, Stoke's Scottish midfielder, picked up the ball 60 metres from goal and fired a perfect, swerving, left-foot shot that burned itself immediately into Premier League history.

This was not the only impact it had. A minute later, at half-time, Mourinho brought on Costa for Oscar. And 11 minutes after that, Costa collapsed, holding his hamstring. The repetition of the injury late in the season was startlingly similar to Costa's experience at Atlético, the situation Mourinho himself had raised after Costa could not complete the game against Hull.

Now Mourinho had questions to answer, and he confirmed the balance of the game had been the key influence on his decision.

"If the result was 2-0 he wouldn't play. But I have to risk. My medical department had to risk," said Mourinho. "If the medical department decide to take four weeks, it wouldn't happen. But no way am I upset with my medical department and I am not unhappy with the will of the player to try and help the team.

"From all the scans two days ago, the muscle and the image was completely clean. The player trained twice at 100%. He did much more in training than he did in the match.

"The medical department do fantastic things for us. We will wait for Diego again. Next week Loic [Remy] or Didier [Drogba] will play."

Chelsea's inexorable march to their first league title in five years continued in Costa's absence. A 1-0 win against Queens Park Rangers courtesy of a Fàbregas strike three minutes from the end – on an afternoon in which they did not have one shot on target until the Spaniard's winning strike – was not likely to make the purists quiver, but it moved them seven points clear at the top.

Prior to the QPR game, Mourinho had been asked if Costa would play again before the end of the season. He said: "Certainly. For sure. But I'm not concerned, not concerned. I don't want to think about it for two or three weeks, until he's ready to play. That's my approach. I'm not going to cry about it until he can play. You know, I think we have eight matches to play. If he plays four, it's normal. If he plays three, it's a little bit below what I'm expecting. If he plays five, it's more than I'm expecting."

A single-goal victory at Stamford Bridge over Manchester United, in which Hazard scored, stretched their lead to 10 points and by the time they ground out a 0-0 draw with Arsenal on April 26 – after starting with no recognised striker – it was a matter of when, not if, they would lift the Premier League trophy. A 3-1 win over Leicester on April 29 left them needing just one win to clinch it.

By Mourinho's previous statement, Costa should have been in contention for the visit of Crystal Palace on May 3, when their coronation was due to be confirmed. However, in his pre-match press conference he confirmed that his striker would not be risked and may not kick another ball for the rest of the season. Mourinho said: "There is a chance he might not [play again this season]. If we win Sunday, I would say he doesn't play against Liverpool.

"If we don't win on Sunday and we need points against Liverpool, I'd say he would play. It's about result after result, and our needs. If we don't need him, he probably doesn't play."

As it turned out, another single-goal victory and another strike from the club's Player of the Year, Hazard – the Belgian heading in the rebound from his own missed penalty – secured the league title for Chelsea.

It was an emotional afternoon at Stamford Bridge, giving Mourinho his third title and his first in his second spell at the club. Costa joined in the on-pitch celebrations afterwards, his name being met with raucous cheers, as he emerged with his jeans and a Chelsea top on, to take a bow in front of the fans.

It was expected to be the last Stamford Bridge would see of their star striker that season, but he appeared seven days later – not on the pitch this time, but in the stand, sitting among the fans for Chelsea's 1-1 draw with Liverpool. With a black baseball cap on, chewing a piece of gum and grinning broadly, he was picked out by the Sky cameras in the Upper East Stand as he posed for selfies and gave everyone the thumbs-up, before stewards eventually shepherded him out. It marked another key moment in the growing love affair between Costa and the fans.

"I thought that was fantastic... what the club's security staff thought about it, I don't know," laughed Tim Rolls, chairman of the Chelsea Supporters Association. "He obviously feels a connection with the fans. In the days of selfie sticks and tourist fans, it's quite a thing to do. The Chelsea fans have sung 'Diego, Diego' from day one. There was a few attempts to sing 'Diego Costa, he's a fucking monster' but that didn't take off. I don't like the word legend but I think he could go on to be one.

"He's a different type of player, more like the sort you would get back in the 60s and 70s. We needed a goalscorer and we've got that with Costa. He winds up refs, he winds up opponents, he is very demonstrative on the pitch and the fans took to him from day one. From talking to other fans before he arrived, we were expecting a physical, belligerent centre-forward. We would have been very disappointed if he had been an Olivier Giroud-type, strolling around the pitch. You get the impression that Costa enjoys the club and the whole buzz of the place.

"Ossie [Peter Osgood] had an edge and he was the ultimate in terms of having a connection with the fans. There's been players like John Terry, Zola, Frank Lampard – but it's a long time since we've had a player not just as committed but also as raw as Costa."

So, league won and season over for Costa? Not quite. For a player whose previous 18 months had been bedevilled by hamstring trouble, there seemed little reason for him to appear again in a Chelsea shirt until the club's pre-season.

However, on May 18, six games after limping off against Stoke on April 4, the Chelsea striker started against West Brom at The Hawthorns. It was to be an eventful evening in the West Midlands, with Costa at the heart of controversy once more. Saido Berahino opened the scoring for the home side after nine minutes, but just before the half-hour mark the game took a decisive turn. Fàbregas took possession on the left-hand side of the West Brom box. Costa and West Brom's Gareth McAuley started wrestling in the centre, which led to the Spanish international appearing to grab the defender around the neck. A square-off ensured and as more players got involved, referee Mike Jones showed Costa a yellow card, his eighth of the campaign.

As Jones restored order to the situation, Fàbregas kicked the ball from 20 yards away and struck West Brom's Chris Brunt on the side of the head. Darren Fletcher, the West Brom midfielder, charged over to confront Fàbregas and Jones showed the Spaniard a red card, his first since 2006.

Berahino's penalty and a Brunt strike after the break consigned Chelsea to only their third league defeat of the season. Mourinho was incensed afterwards, particularly on hearing that Fàbregas would be suspended for three games, including the final game of the season and the first two of the 2015-16 campaign.

"Three-game ban for this? Jesus Christ!" said the Chelsea boss. "Harsh? Of course it's harsh, if you get three games for that. For me a top referee, a big personality in control of the game has two or three words and it is done. It was nothing special. One of the top referees would resolve the problem with words. Jones gave the red card, which I disagree completely with, but he is the referee."

However, Mourinho was quick to turn the focus of the incident onto West Brom's treatment of Costa, with Jonas Olsson and Craig Gardner both having been booked for fouls on him.

"Of course he was [targeted]," said Mourinho. "But I don't want to repeat the same story. You have to speak more about the opponents than Costa. If you see what they did to him from the first minute, it is easy to understand there are other people to blame. It depends on the referee. If the referee wants to protect the talent and punish the bully it is easy for him."

By starting Costa against West Brom, Mourinho had also partly contradicted his previous statement that "it's about result after result, and our needs... if we don't need him, he probably doesn't play."

Chelsea didn't need him, but he still played. Why?

Mourinho: "He wants to play. He is completely responsible. For me I would keep working without playing but he is desperate to play. He has felt good the last couple of weeks and he begged me to play him."

Similar to the 2014 Champions League final and Diego Simeone's change of heart – although with significantly less at stake – Costa had persuaded another hard-nosed manager that he should play despite risk of injury.

Inevitably, Costa also featured in the club's final league game of the season, a 3-1 win over Sunderland, when he converted a penalty before half-time to cancel out Steven Fletcher's opener. It brought the curtain down on a remarkable season for Costa and Chelsea. The title winners had finished on 87 points, eight clear of second-placed Manchester City, having lost just three league games and conceded 33 goals.

As Mourinho pointed out, the player's rehabilitation would continue over the summer months. "We are preparing a good working situation for him during the holiday period, where he can obviously mix the holiday with work."

The season had followed a similar trajectory for Costa to his previous campaign – an incredible start followed by an injury-blighted end. However, the stats spoke volumes for his impact – 20 goals in 26 starts. Chelsea had found their new Drogba. A club who had fallen in love with the wrecking-ball style of the Ivorian over the previous decade were always likely to succumb to a striker of Costa's ilk.

Pat Nevin, who played over 250 games for the Stamford Bridge side during the 1980s, has not been not slow to recognise the dawn of a new Chelsea hero. Just four league games into his Chelsea career, Nevin wrote in his column on the Chelsea website: "I don't use the word legend often, some bandy it about with abandon, but in many ways it should be kept sacred, not treated lightly. Legends are the likes of Osgood, Zola, Terry, Drogba and Lampard. There are many, but not that many and to enter that pantheon it takes years' worth of quality at the very highest level, so be restrained. It can take players years into their time at a club to be considered in that bracket and that is the way it should be. Even so, it seems clear to me that our new striker has everything to grab a place in our house for historical heroes. To do so, he has to stay at the club, stay fit and stay hungry, and have long periods of good form.

"It is a lot to ask, but now and again we get a feeling for a player at Stamford Bridge and already he feels like family, indeed he feels like a favoured son. Long may it continue."

Nevin expanded on the fusion of talent and personality which he thinks will see Costa secure his place in the pantheon. "Chelsea fans love big personalities. Osgood was a big personality. Costa seems to care about the club. Over the years, Chelsea fans have been fantastic to me – they're a very passionate bunch. When they take someone to their heart, they're never forgotten. When I scored against Chelsea while playing for Everton I was applauded off the park. With Costa, I think even the injuries have endeared him. He's clearly not been 100% at times, but he is the type who you need to tell him he's not fit to play rather than plead with him to play. Fans get that.

"He will be here for the long haul."

REFERENCES

CHAPTER 1

The Street Footballer

Diego Costa was talking about what he learned on the streets of Lagarto to Mónica Marchante on Canal Plus

CHAPTER 3

Celta Vigo: The Good, the Bad and the Ugly

Costa was discussing the difference in what is acceptable in pro football compared to the games he played as a youth in *El País*

CHAPTER 7

Rayo Vallecano: The Reprieve

Costa talked about the importance of his final loan move to Eleonora Giovio, of *El País*

CHAPTER 8

Atlético: Kings of the Bernabéu

Diego Simeone spoke to Canal Plus about initially choosing Toto over Costa for his final non-EU slot

Costa lauded Radamel Falcao in an interview with Gol Television

And he was talking to *Four Four Two* about his 'strategy' of winding up opponents

CHAPTER 9

Partido a Partido

Mundo Deportivo journalist Jesús Hernández was talking to Costa about finally getting the chance to be the man at Atléti.

Simeone was talking to *El País* about his growing appreciation of Costa's game

The coach's reflections on his decision to play Costa in the big games at the end of the season, and his injuries, come from his own autobiography

Costa's final reflection on the season came in an interview with *MC News*

CHAPTER 10

An International Incident

Costa talked openly about his switch to Spain in an interview to journalist Mónica Marchante

And he reflected on his Spain debut with Matías Prats from *Telecinco*

Vicente Del Bosque was analysing what went wrong in *El País*

CHAPTER 11

Chelsea: Going to War

Alan Shearer and Phil Neville were enthusing about Costa on the BBC's *Match of the Day*

Gary Neville spoke to Jose Mourinho in *The Daily Telegraph*

And Neville defended Costa after the Liverpool game in his column for the same newspaper

INDEX

B

C

ALSO AVAILABLE FROM

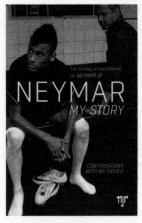

NEYMAR: MY STORY
CONVERSATIONS WITH MY
FATHER

'fascinating insights'
Daily Mail

'moving and informative'
Sunday Mirror

I remember it like it was yesterday. It was 23 August 2010. My father and I had a meeting with president Luis Álvaro at the Santos headquarters inside Vila Belmiro. Chelsea had made a huge offer for me.

In the middle of our conversation, the president turned off the lights and pointed at an empty chair. 'This chair belong to the nation's greatest sporting hero. Since Ayrton Senna's death, this chair has sat vacant. If Neymar Jr turns down Chelsea's offer and stays at Santos, he will have taken his first step towards sitting there.'

Everyone was very tense at that meeting, because it was my future on that table. That decision would be a turning point in my life, whichever way it turned out. Pelé even called me. Can you imagine how important I felt? The King called and asked me to stay. He reminded me that he had spent his entire competitive career with Santos, he had won major trophies with the club and he had established his legend with the Seleção while playing for Santos. Of course, it was a different time, a different world, a different football. We considered all of that as we pondered our final decision.

A few months earlier, Pep had said to his closest colleagues: "I know Mourinho and he's trying to provoke me into a reaction, but it won't work. I'm not going to react. I'm not going to answer back. Only when I think the time is right."

Now his moment had come. At 8pm on the day before the match, the players left the training session at the Bernabéu, sensing that Pep was about to respond to Mourinho.

"Señor Mourinho has permitted himself the luxury of calling me Pep, so I will call him Jose," he said. "Tomorrow at 8.45pm we face each other on the pitch. He has won the battle off the pitch. If he wants his own personal Champions League trophy away from the pitch, let him take it home and enjoy it. In this room [the Bernabéu press room] Mourinho is the f------ chief, the f------ boss. He knows all about this and I don't want to compete with him in here. I'd just like to remind him that I worked with him for four years [at Barcelona]. He knows me and I know him. If he prefers to value the views of the journalist friends who take their information in a drip feed from Florentino Pérez more than the relationship we had for four years then that's his choice. I try to learn from Jose on the pitch, but I prefer to learn as little as possible from him off the pitch."

Pep's response had inflamed an already tense situation. When he arrived at the team hotel, his men were waiting to give him a standing ovation. They considered the response long overdue.

ALSO AVAILABLE FROM

THE SECRET AGENT
INSIDE THE WORLD OF THE
FOOTBALL AGENT

'stellar … exposes the truth about the life
of football's middle men'
Daily Telegraph

*I always knew I wanted to do something in football, just like I always knew I
wanted to be rich. The trouble was that, as a kid, I was pretty crap on the pitch,
and when you come from an East London council estate with parents who both
have to work for a living, then the odds are really stacked against you.*

*So, ruling out being the next David Beckham, or buying my own club,
that left me with fairly limited choices. But then I watched a programme that
changed my life. Or at least made me make a life-changing decision. It was
one of those fly-on-the-wall documentaries that was meant to uncover the dirt
and corruption that lay beneath the world of football agents. You know the
sort of thing, paying bungs to managers to make a deal happen, fitting up a
rival to steal a player, lying through their teeth to parents to get the first run on
looking after little Tommy and, worst of all (at least as far as the programme
makers were concerned), making serious money.*

*Now, I know that to most people that would be a turn-off. Who wants to
be a part of what seemed to be one of the most reviled groups of operators in
the world? Yet, at twenty years of age, it seemed more of an opportunity than
a turn-off.*

ALSO AVAILABLE FROM

A glance at the official squad lists for the World Cup showed that the most represented club within the Seleção was Chelsea, with four out 23 players, followed by Barcelona and Paris St. Germain, both with two. Germany, on the other hand, brought seven Bayern Munich players, six of them first team regulars, followed by four Borussia Dortmund players. Moreover, 16 out of the 23 players were based in the Bundesliga. Group familiarity was much more prevalent among Die Nationalmannschaft and emphasised still further when 15 of the players called up by Joachim Löw had more than 20 caps for their country, five more than Brazil.

Brazil were missing their captain and their star attacking player so everything suggested they should adopt a conservative approach for the game in Belo Horizonte. Big Phil added more mystery to proceedings by putting a variety of formations in place in the practice sessions before the game. In the last one, on 6 July, Brazil used no less than six variations of style and personnel. But in his pre-match press conference, Scolari remained stoic. 'We need to respect Germany but we cannot refrain from trying to impose our game,' he said.

ALSO AVAILABLE FROM

BACKPAGE

BARÇA
THE MAKING OF THE GREATEST TEAM IN THE WORLD

Football Book of the Year – British Sports Book Awards

Book of the Year – Football Supporters, Federation Awards

'A superbly written analysis and celebration of Pep, Messi, Xavi, etc. A brilliant book'
Henry Winter, *The Daily Telegraph*

'An instant classic' *Sports Illustrated*

If the 175,000 FC Barcelona members, or socios, queued up in an orderly line, night after night, to massage his tired feet, cook his dinner and tuck him into bed; if they carried his golf clubs round Montanya's hilly 18 holes; if they devoted 50% of their annual salary to him … it still wouldn't be anywhere near enough to repay the debt those who love this club owe Johan Cruyff.

Without him, there would be no Pep Guardiola, no Messi, no Xavi and no Andrés Iniesta. They would have been judged to be too slow, too small – table footballers. The genius from Amsterdam created the conditions which allowed these incredible players to be recognised and to become central to FC Barcelona's values. Without Cruyff, this story simply wouldn't exist.

ALSO AVAILABLE FROM

BACKPAGE

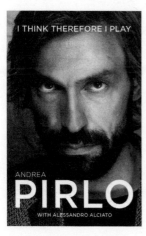

ANDREA PIRLO
I THINK THEREFORE I PLAY

'Pirlo's book is the most eloquent, funny footballer's memoirs in years'
Sam Wallace, *The Independent*

'Pirlo's autobiography is ... like an erotic novel for football fans.' *****
Four Four Two

'*I Think Therefore I Play* ... displays a mischievous wit and an acute gift for observation'
Richard Williams, *The Guardian*

After the wheel, the PlayStation is the best invention of all time. And ever since it's existed, I've been Barcelona, apart from a brief spell way back at the start when I'd go Milan. I can't say with any certainty how many virtual matches I've played over the last few years but, roughly speaking, it must be at least four times the number of real ones. Pirlo v Nesta was a classic duel back in our Milanello days. We'd get in early, have breakfast at 9am and then shut ourselves in our room and hit the PlayStation until 11. Training would follow, then we'd be back on the computer games until four in the afternoon. Truly a life of sacrifice. Our head-to-heads were pure adrenaline. I'd go Barcelona and so would Sandro. Barca v Barca. The first player I'd pick was the quickest one, Samuel Eto'o, but I'd still end up losing a lot of the time. I'd get pissed off and hurl away my controller before asking Sandro for a rematch. And then I'd lose again.